SEEK AND EXPLORE

DEVOTIONS FOR KIDS

365
DAYS OF HANDS-ON ACTIVITIES

Yvonne Van Ee, PhD
Michael Williams, PhD

 ZONDER**kidz**

Introduction

In this devotional, you will be studying one book of the Bible each week. There are 6 days of reading and activities for each book. And guess what? When you are finished with this book, you will understand what God is saying to you in every book of the Bible! And you get to do fun things along the way too! The best way to start each week is to read the summary on day 1. This will give you a good idea of the main idea of the book. Then the next day, move on to day 2. It's that simple and that fun!

Most of the activities for each day can be done on your own. But sometimes we ask you to work with others. They can be your family, friends, or classmates. If you don't have anyone to work with, do your best to complete the activities on your own.

Throughout this book you will meet some animal friends that will help you learn about the Bible. Here is a little more about them:

Arty is a meerkat from southern Africa. She is always seeing pictures and projects in her head.

Crafty is a jaguar from South America. He loves hands-on experiences and is always playing with something or someone.

Greeny is an antelope who has relatives in many parts of the world. She likes to go on wilderness journeys with her binoculars and magnifying glass.

Inny is a tiger from Asia. Inny likes to be on his own. Reading helps him understand what is going on in his head.

Joinme is a hippopotamus from Africa. She is good at making friends and helping groups work together.

Talky is a monkey who has relatives all over the world. He loves to read and learns by talking with his friends.

Thinky is an African elephant who also has relatives in Asia. She is a famous problem solver.

Hummy is a zebra from Africa. She can play any musical instrument you can think of and she sings like an angel.

Hearty is a bear from the northern hemisphere. He understands feelings and loves to give his friends his special bear hug. There are eight colors for eight different feelings or emotions on Hearty's color chart. You will be using the chart for a few activities in this book.

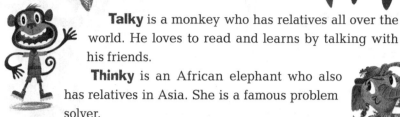

Hearty's color chart

Look at the different colors that **Hearty** loves to use to show his emotions.

Red = Angry   Brown = Boredom
Purple = Rage   Gray = Loneliness
Blue = Sadness   Yellow = Happiness
Green = Jealousy   Orange = Excitement

Hearty will often invite you to choose a color that shows how you are feeling.

Week 1, Day 1

Read About It

**God will bless all nations through
the person he has chosen.**

Do you remember when your life began? Of course not! But it's fun to hear about it, right? Well, everything in the whole wide world begins in the book of Genesis! The sky and earth begin. Human beings begin. Those were good things. But sin begins too. Sin breaks and hurts the good things God began. But God loves us so much, and he has a plan to fix what sin has broken! Genesis tells us about this plan.

This is how sin came into the world. After God created the world, he created the first human beings. Their names were Adam and Eve. Adam and Eve had a perfect relationship with God in the Garden of Eden. But they lost that relationship when the serpent tricked them into sinning against God. Sin breaks things. It broke God's perfect world. It broke Adam and Eve's relationship with God. It also broke Adam and Eve's relationship with each other. But God's love is greater than sin's power! God decided to show his love by fixing his broken world and his broken people. This is God's great blessing for us!

At this point in Genesis, we begin to hear about Abraham. God chose to bring his blessing to the whole world through Abraham and his family. God protected and provided for Abraham's family. You can read the story of Abraham beginning in Genesis 12. Abraham is the man God chose to use to begin fixing the world sin had broken.

6   **The book of Genesis takes place in Mesopotamia, Canaan, and Egypt. Use a map to find these places.**

Think About It

Find the words that tell about people, places, and things in Genesis. They may be written forward, backward, up, down, or at an angle. Use the words listed by the puzzle.

GENESIS

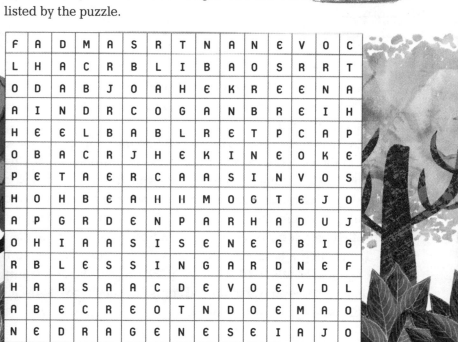

F	A	D	M	A	S	R	T	N	A	N	E	V	O	C
L	H	A	C	R	B	L	I	B	A	O	S	R	R	T
O	D	A	B	J	O	A	H	E	K	R	E	E	N	A
A	I	N	D	R	C	O	G	A	N	B	R	E	I	H
H	E	E	L	B	A	B	L	R	E	T	P	C	A	P
O	B	A	C	R	J	H	E	K	I	N	E	O	K	E
P	E	T	A	E	R	C	A	A	S	I	N	V	O	S
H	O	H	B	E	A	H	H	II	M	O	G	T	E	J	O
A	P	G	R	D	E	N	P	A	R	H	A	D	U	J
O	H	I	A	A	S	I	S	E	N	E	G	B	I	G
R	B	L	E	S	S	I	N	G	A	R	D	N	E	F
H	A	R	S	A	A	C	D	E	V	O	E	V	D	L
A	B	E	C	R	E	O	T	N	D	O	E	M	A	O
N	E	D	R	A	G	E	N	E	S	E	I	A	J	O
T	L	L	E	H	C	A	R	S	E	S	O	J	U	D

Abel	create	Isaac	Pharaoh
Abraham	Eden	Jacob	Rachel
Adam	Eve	Joseph	Rebekah
Babel	flood	Judah	Sarah
blessing	garden	Leah	serpent
Cain	Genesis	light	sin
covenant	God	Noah	

Finding Jesus in Genesis

Read Genesis 12:1–3. What is the main idea of these verses?

....

....

....

God promised Abraham that all nations on earth would be blessed because of him. Jesus came to bring that blessing over a thousand years later.

Now read Matthew 1:1–17. You will find the main idea of these verses in the very first verse. Jesus comes from Abraham's family line, just as God promised so long ago. And Jesus is the one who brings God's blessing to us. Everyone who believes in Jesus is saved from all the brokenness sin has caused. God heals them. Everyone who believes in Jesus receives this promised blessing from God.

Try making a family line for Jesus. Use the line below. Hint: Look again at Matthew 1:1–17 for help. Fill in some famous family members in between Abraham and Jesus. You don't have to list all of them because there are quite a few!

|————————————————————————————————|

ABRAHAM   JESUS

Write About It

Read Genesis 12:2–3. Write here the number of times God uses the words "I will" in his promise. _____ This number means God's promised blessing is very important to him. God wants you to know that his promised blessing is for you.

In your own words write the blessing that God has promised.

....

....

....

....

....

....

....

....

....

....

Week 1, Day 5

Pray About It

Loving God,

Thank you that you love me even though I sinned against you. Thank you that you wanted me to know how wonderful life could be with you. Thank you for sending Jesus to fix what sin has broken. Thank you for sending Jesus to do that for me. Because of Jesus I can be your friend forever. Please help me to live in a way that shows how much I love you. I pray these things because I believe in Jesus.
Amen.

What are you thankful for?

....

....

....

....

How can you live in a way that shows how much you love God?

....

....

....

....

Week 1, Day 6

Do Something About It

GENESIS

God chose Abraham to be the person who would bring his blessing to the nations. That blessing came through Jesus Christ. He was born into Abraham's family line. When we believe in Jesus, God gives each one of us a special purpose too. This special purpose is for you to be a blessing to others. You do this when you tell them about the blessing God wants to give them too. That is how God's blessing goes out to the whole world!

Plan for how you can do this. First, what should you do to get ready? Ask your parents or pastor to help you think of words to say or things to do. They could also help you find helpful Bible verses.

Second, think of a person or group of people you want to know about your blessing. Draw a picture of them.

Third, how will you be a blessing? Remember, this doesn't always mean talking to others. It can be doing things for other people that will show them what a true follower of Jesus is like.

I will:

11

Week 2, Day 1

Read About It

God saves his people from sin so they can have a wonderful life with him.

Well, this wasn't supposed to happen! Abraham's family had become the nation of Israel. They were living in the land of Egypt. But Pharaoh, the ruler of Egypt, had made them his slaves. This wasn't what God had promised to Abraham and his family line! God had promised to bless them. Did Pharaoh have the power to stop God's blessing from happening? Pharaoh was acting like he thought he could! God would have to show him he was very, very wrong.

God sent Moses to tell Pharaoh to let the Israelites go. But Pharaoh refused. That was a big mistake! God sent 10 horrible plagues to Egypt to get Pharaoh to change his mind. After the last plague, Pharaoh finally let the Israelites go. But guess what! Pharaoh changed his mind and chased after them! He caught up with them at the Red Sea. The Israelites were trapped! There was water in front of them and Pharaoh's army behind them! But God rescued them by making a dry path through the water. Then God caused the sea to flow back over the Egyptians. They couldn't follow the Israelites anymore. The Israelites were free at last!

But God doesn't just save his people from harm. God also saves his people so they can be his children. Being a child of God is the very best life there is!

The book of Exodus mostly takes place in Egypt and Canaan. These are in the modern-day countries of Egypt, Israel, and Jordan. Use a map to find these places.

Think About It

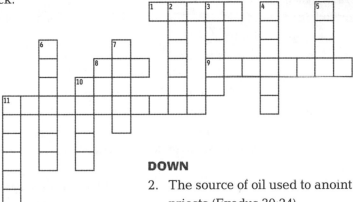

This crossword puzzle will help you to learn important people, places, and events in Exodus.

Each clue also has a verse to look up if you get stuck.

DOWN

2. The source of oil used to anoint priests (Exodus 30:24)
3. The country where the people of Israel were held as slaves (Exodus 3:7)
4. The water the people of Israel crossed when they left Egypt (Exodus 15:22)
5. The main river of Egypt (Exodus 7:15)
6. The title for the ruler of Egypt (Exodus 3:10)
7. The second plague God sent to Egypt (Exodus 8:2)
10. The mountain where Moses received God's law (Exodus 19:20)
11. What the ruler of Egypt forced the people of Israel to make without straw (Exodus 5:7)

ACROSS

1. The man God used to lead his people out of Egypt (Exodus 3:10–11)
8. The box where the Ten Commandments were kept (Exodus 25:16, 22)
9. The day the people of Israel celebrate being saved from Egypt (Exodus 12:11)
11. The plant where God called Moses in the desert (Exodus 3:2)

EXODUS

13

Finding Jesus in Exodus

Pharaoh was cruel. He refused to set the Israelites free. So, God sent the worst plague of all. He killed all the boys in Egypt that were born first to their mothers. This included Pharaoh's own child. Even the male animals born first died that night. But all the boys born first among Israelite families did not die! God protected his children.

God told the Israelites to sacrifice their best lambs. Then they had to wipe the blood on the doorframes of their houses. That night God moved over the land of Egypt. He killed the Egyptian boys born first in their families. But he skipped over the Israelite houses. That's because he saw the blood they had put on their doors. That night became known as the first Passover. It is a yearly Jewish holiday that celebrates this event.

Hundreds of years later Jesus was crucified on the cross. He was like a lamb whose blood protects God's people. Jesus was the perfect sacrifice for all humankind. Because he gave his blood, we are free from the punishment of sin.

The Lord will fight for you. Just be still.

—Exodus 14:14

Write About It

Read Exodus 29:46. What reason does God give in this verse for saving his people?

....

God lives with everyone who believes in Jesus. How does that make you feel? Choose one of the colors from Hearty's color chart. Then tell why you chose that color.

....

....

....

Think of a few things you can do to remind yourself that God lives with you. Write them here.

....

....

....

Week 2, Day 5

Pray About It

Dear God,

Thank you that you have saved me from sin. Sin breaks things and makes everything it touches bad. But you are more powerful than sin. You are the only one who is! You have saved me from sin's power. Thank you for wanting to live with me. And thank you that because I believe in Jesus Christ you do live with me! Your Holy Spirit helps me understand how to live. You show me the wonderful life you want for me. Please help me remember that you live with me. I ask you for this because I believe in Jesus.
Amen.

Now think about how you have sinned and been forgiven. Write down some sins that you need to remember so you won't repeat them.

My Sins

....

....

....

....

....

How I Remember that God Lives with Me

....

....

....

....

Do Something About It

God has set us free from the evil power of sin. We can live because of what Jesus has done for us. When we trust in Jesus, we become God's children. Then sin doesn't control us anymore, God does! God gives us instructions in the Bible about how to live. When we follow the instructions, our lives will be the best they can be!

This verse from the book of Galatians reviews the message of Exodus. Rewrite this verse in the space below like a work of art. You can create fancy letters and add pictures.

> Christ has set us free to enjoy our freedom. So remain strong in the faith. Don't let the chains of slavery hold you again.
>
> GALATIANS 5:1

17

Week 3, Day 1

Read About It

**God shows his people how to be holy
so that they can live with him.**

Have you ever walked on a clean floor with dirty shoes? The person who cleaned the floor was probably not too happy about that! You must have clean shoes to walk on a clean floor. And you must have a clean heart to live with God. In other words, you must be holy because God is holy. By bringing offerings to God, his people could become holy.

There were five kinds of offerings, and they each did a different thing. The people brought the first kind of offering to show God how much they loved him. They brought the second kind to thank God for giving them life. The third kind of offering said they wanted to be friends with God. They brought the fourth kind of offering if they had sinned against God. This offering was a way to say they were sorry for sinning against him. They brought the fifth kind of offering if they had turned away from God. This offering was a way to say they wanted to come back to him.

These offerings were a way for the Israelites to stay close to God. He is perfect and pure. But his people make mistakes. They aren't perfect or pure. But God wants to live with his people always. He gave them these offerings as a way to pay for their mistakes. Then God could live with them always.

Think of some ways that you can offer God thanks, love, friendship, and say you're sorry for your sins.

18

Think About It

In the reading, we learned that the Israelites offered five kinds of offerings. Each offering did a different thing. To learn the names of these five offerings, unscramble the letters of each one below.

1. NRTBU __ __ __ __ __ __
   See Leviticus 1:3 for a clue. A person brought this offering to show God how much they loved him.

2. ANGIR __ __ __ __ __
   See Leviticus 2:1 for a clue. A person brought this offering to say thank you to God for giving them life.

3. PIDFRSHINE __ __ __ __ __ __ __ __ __ __
   See Leviticus 3:1 for a clue. A person brought this offering to say they always wanted to be friends with God.

4. NSI __ __ __
   See Leviticus 4:3 for a clue. A person brought this offering to say they were sorry for sinning against God.

5. ILUTG __ __ __ __ __
   See Leviticus 5:15 for a clue. A person brought this offering to say they wanted to come back to God.

LEVITICUS

Week 3, Day 3

Finding Jesus in Leviticus

The five kinds of offerings in Leviticus had to be given all the time. But God sent Jesus to do everything these sacrifices did! And Jesus is an offering that never has to be given again!

The first kind of offering was burned up completely. Jesus offers himself completely to God for us. So, when we believe in Jesus we belong completely to God.

The second kind of offering was a way to say thank you to God. That's because God provides food to live. God gives us eternal life when we believe in Jesus.

A person brought the third kind of offering to say they always wanted to be friends with God. When we believe in Jesus, we're God's friends forever.

A person brought the fourth kind of offering to say they were sorry for hurting God. We hurt God when we sin. Jesus covers over all our sins when we believe in him.

The fifth kind of offering tells God we want to come back to him. We never want to leave him again! When we believe in Jesus, we will be God's children forever!

There are five offerings and five letters in the name **Jesus**. Color each letter in the name Jesus a different color to stand for each kind of offering.

20

Week 3, Day 4

Write About It

Jesus has done what all the offerings in Leviticus did. But the offerings in Leviticus had to be given over and over again. What Jesus has done lasts forever! How does that make you feel? Choose a color from Hearty's color chart and write why you chose that color.

....

....

....

Suppose you were invited to spend some time with the most important person in the world? How would you feel? Guess what? God is so much greater than any person on earth! He is holy and pure, and he has made you his child! You can spend time with him always. Write how that makes you feel.

....

....

....

Hearty's color chart

Red = Angry
Purple = Rage
Blue = Sadness
Green = Jealousy

Brown = Boredom
Gray = Loneliness
Yellow = Happiness
Orange = Excitement

21

Week 3, Day 5

Pray About It

Dear God,

You are holy and pure. I know that I can't be holy and pure on my own. Thank you for sending your Son to be an offering for me. He paid the price for my mistakes so that you can forgive me. Jesus is holy and he makes me holy in your eyes. Now I can be your child forever. Help me to remember what you've done for me. Please make me more like Jesus. Then I can know more about this wonderful life. I ask you for this because I believe in Jesus.

Amen.

Jesus shows us how to live a holy life. Think of some ways that you can be more like Jesus. Draw your ideas in the box below.

Week 3, Day 6

Do Something About It

It is easy to forget that God is holy. Sometimes we think God is like us. But God is perfect and we aren't.

Here is something you can do to remind yourself of these things.

Be holy, because I am holy. I am the LORD your God.
LEVITICUS 19:2

Create a book about holiness. Fold several sheets of regular paper in half. Staple at the fold to hold them together. On the cover, write the words of Leviticus 19:2 (see above). Then look up the verses written below in your NIrV Bible. Write them in your book. Look up the definition of "holy" and write it in your own words. Ask a pastor or a Christian friend what they think holiness means. Add their definitions to your book. Keep this project close by to help you remember that God is holy. And it will help you remember that we should try to be holy too.

Leviticus 20:26

1 Samuel 2:2

Ezekiel 38:23

2 Timothy 1:9

Hebrews 12:4

1 Peter 1:15-16

Week 4, Day 1

Read About It

**God punishes his people when they disobey.
But he will keep his promise to bless them.**

You've probably disobeyed your parents at one time or another. Maybe you thought you knew better than they did. Maybe you just didn't want to do what they said. It probably didn't turn out so well for you. Parents know what they're talking about! They tell you what to do because they want what is best for you.

God was like a parent to the Israelites. He saved them from Egypt. He protected them and provided for them in the desert. Then he told them to enter the land he had promised them. But they were afraid! There were strong people living there! The Israelites thought maybe God wouldn't be able to do what he had promised. They stopped trusting him. They were going to disobey him. They forgot God was more powerful than anything they were afraid of.

God reminded his people how important it was to believe him. God would still give his people the land. But they would have to wait until their children grew up. That was a long time! Then the Israelites would finally get the land if they trusted and obeyed God.

Have you ever been afraid to do something that you knew was right? Why were you afraid to do it?

Think About It

Unscramble the names of important people in the book of Numbers. Then unscramble the circled letters of each unscrambled name. When you do this, you will find the name of another important person in the book.

NUMBERS

1. This person was one of the men who gave a good report about the promised land. Read Numbers 13:30 for a clue.

   1. BLEAC

2. This is the person who would replace Moses as the leader of God's people. Read Numbers 27:18 for a clue.

   2. SHOUJA

3. This person's name appears in the first and last verses of the book of Numbers. Read Numbers 36:13 for a clue.

   3. SOMES

4. In this valley, the men who checked out the land cut off a bunch of grapes. Read Numbers 13:24 for a clue.

   4. HOLEKS

5. This is one of the men who turned against Moses in the wilderness. Read Numbers 16:1 for a clue.

   5. HOARK

6. Unscramble the circled letters from above to solve the riddle below.

   What is the name of the man who rode on a donkey and tried to put a curse on the people of Israel?

25

Week 4, Day 3

Finding Jesus in Numbers

The Israelites had trouble trusting and obeying God. If only they had trusted him, they would have enjoyed his blessing! Do you have trouble trusting and obeying God too? We all do. If only we could trust and obey God all the time! Then we would never have to worry that we were missing out on God's blessing.

God wants us to have his blessing too. That's why he sent his own son, Jesus. Jesus always trusted and obeyed God perfectly. And when we believe in Jesus, here is what happens. God counts what Jesus did as what we did! And God counts Jesus' suffering as payment for all the times we don't trust and obey. So, we don't have to miss out on any of God's blessings anymore. Jesus has made sure that we can have God's blessing forever. Thank you, Jesus!

How good are you at trusting God? Rate yourself by circling a number below (5 is best).

1   2   3   4   5

Do you have a hard time trusting God? Explain your answer.

....

....

....

Week 4, Day 4

Write About It

NUMBERS

Imagine you were one of the Israelites who heard the report about the promised land. You heard about the powerful and super scary people. You heard about the large cities with high walls around them. Do you think you would have wanted to go into that land? Write your thoughts here.

....

....

....

The Israelites disobeyed because they didn't believe God could do what he promised. They were afraid of the people in the land. But Caleb reminded them that God was with them. God was more powerful than what they were afraid of. Think about what you're afraid of. God is with you too and is more powerful than what you're afraid of. Write how that makes you feel.

....

....

....

27

Week 4, Day 5

Pray About It

Dear God,

You always keep your promises. Sometimes I forget them or don't believe them. But you keep loving me anyway. Thank you for sending Jesus to pay the price for all the times I disobey. Thank you for sending your Spirit to help me trust you and obey you. Please help me do this more and more. I ask you for this because I believe in Jesus.
Amen.

In what ways can you obey and trust God more? Write them here.

....

....

....

What promises has God kept in your life? Write them in the Bible below.

Do Something About It

Sometimes *doing* something helps us remember better than *reading* something. Here is something you can do. It will help you remember that God will always guide you and keep you on the right path.

You may want an older person to help you with this. Make sure you get permission. Take a ruler or yardstick and lay it on a table. Prop one end of the ruler or yardstick on top of a book so that it is at an angle. Now take a hardboiled or plastic egg and place it at the top of the ruler or yardstick. You can even use a raw egg if you dare! The goal is to have the egg roll all the way down to the bottom without falling off the side. You're going to have to watch that egg closely! If you don't keep it on track with your hands, it will roll off and crack open! It could be a huge mess!

That is an example of what God does with us. He guides us through life by what he says in the Bible. When we let him keep us on track, we'll be safe. If we refuse to listen to him, we'll go sailing off in the wrong direction. And we could end up broken, just like the egg. Anytime you think God can't be trusted or if you think about disobeying him, just remember the egg. Without God guiding us on the path of life, we would make a mess of things too.

Week 5, Day 1

Read About It

God tells his people how to have the best life possible in the promised land.

Imagine wandering around in a hot and dusty desert for 40 years! That is exactly what Moses and the Israelites did. All during that time God provided for them. He gave them manna to eat and water to drink. And God taught the Israelites what they must do to live with him. He gave them instructions about how to worship him. He gave them rules about how to live their daily lives. God used Moses to teach the Israelites his rules and commands. Together Moses and the Israelites learned how to live as God's chosen people. The Israelites learned that they could have a wonderful life with God. But to have this life, they must keep God's commands. If they did, God promised to live among them and bless them. But God's people always had trouble living as he instructed.

In this book Moses comes to the end of his life. He knows the Israelites have not followed God's commands perfectly. So, he wants to remind the Israelites once more about what is most important. Moses reminds the Israelites of who God is and his promise to them. He reminds them of their special relationship with God. He reminds the Israelites to obey the rules and commands God gave them. Obeying these rules and commands will bring them the best life possible. It is a life lived in relationship with God.

The events in the book of Deuteronomy take place near the Jordan River. Use a map to find its location.

Think About It

The commandments are listed below. The benefits of the commandments are listed as well. Write the letter of the benefit on the line next to the commandment it describes.

_____ Do not put any other gods in place of me.

_____ Do not make statues of other gods to worship.

_____ Do not misuse the name of the Lord your God.

_____ Keep the Sabbath day holy.

_____ Honor your father and mother.

_____ Do not murder.

_____ Respect the promises of marriage.

_____ Do not steal.

_____ Do not say untrue things about your neighbor.

_____ Do not want to have anything your neighbor owns.

a. I get to worship God every Sunday with other believers.

b. God keeps his promises. I will keep my promises to others.

c. God has made me his child. He is my God and has the most special place in my heart.

d. God has shown me what is true and right. I will only say true and right things.

e. God gave his own Son as a gift to me. So, I won't take what belongs to other people.

f. God is so great. I will worship nothing but him.

g. We are all made to be like God. I would never do anything to harm anyone.

h. God is holy and perfect. I will use his name with respect.

i. God has given me everything I need. I don't want what other people have.

j. God has given me people who love and care for me. I am thankful for them.

DEUTERONOMY

31

Week 5, Day 3

Finding Jesus in Deuteronomy

God's people often forget about the wonderful life he has promised for them. They forget that God's rules and commands tell them how to have that best life possible. So, they forget to keep those rules and commands. When we don't keep God's rules and commands, our lives don't turn out well. Not only that, our relationship with God isn't everything it could be.

God sent his son, Jesus. He perfectly kept God's rules and commands. When we believe in Jesus, his obedience is counted as our obedience. And because of what Jesus did, God's relationship with us can never be broken.

The Holy Spirit helps anyone who believes in Jesus become more like Jesus. This means that believers will try to follow God's rules and commands just as Jesus did. These rules and instructions show the believer how to have the best life possible. That life comes from having a relationship with God. Believers will want to say thank you to God for that life. Following God's rules and commands is the way to do that.

God gives you the best life possible when you believe in Jesus. How can you show God you are thankful for that life? Remember, you are trying to be more like Jesus.

Week 5, Day 4

Write About It

Our sin breaks our relationship with God. But Jesus obeyed God's commands perfectly so we can have a relationship with God again. When you believe in Jesus, God sends his Spirit to you. The Holy Spirit helps you live the way God wants. Choose a color from Hearty's color chart to show how that makes you feel. Then write about why you chose that color.

....

....

....

We know we do not obey God's commands perfectly. But God wants us to use them to guide the way we live. When we do, we live the way God wants. Read again the list of God's commandments. Choose one commandment you want to especially remember. Write why it is important to you.

Commandment:

....

Why it is important:

....

....

....

....

....

33

DEUTERONOMY

Pray About It

Loving God,

Thank you for sending Jesus to me. Thank you that he kept your commands perfectly. Thank you for sending your Holy Spirit to me. Please help me to obey your commands because I love you. I know that following your commands will lead to the best life possible! I want to learn and follow them more faithfully. I pray this because I believe in Jesus. Amen.

Look at the path. Write ways that you can obey God's commands.

Do Something About It

In Day 4 of Deuteronomy you chose one commandment you wanted to especially remember. In Day 2 you learned about the benefit of that commandment. What does the benefit of that commandment make you think about? Draw a picture of what that looks like. Make it colorful.

DEUTERONOMY

Week 6, Day 1

Read About It

God gives his people rest after leading them to win their battles.

Learning to ride a bike can be exciting. But it can be scary too! Sometimes you need someone to help you keep the bike from falling over.

The Israelites had a scary thing they needed to do too. They needed to enter the land God had promised to give them. But other people were already living on that land. To get their land, God told the Israelites they would have to fight for it! Israel couldn't do this scary thing unless God helped them. But God promised to be right there beside them. God would fight for them! And no one in the whole world can fight against God and win!

Joshua led the Israelites in all their battles. But it was God who gave them victory. If they trusted God, he would make sure they would win. Sometimes it seemed better to trust in other things. But the Israelites learned that trusting in God is always best. That's how they won their battles. After they won their battles, the Israelites made their home in the promised land. They thanked God that now they could live in peace and rest.

The book of Joshua was written to help God's followers remember to trust and obey him. What are some things that help you remember to trust and obey God?

Think About It

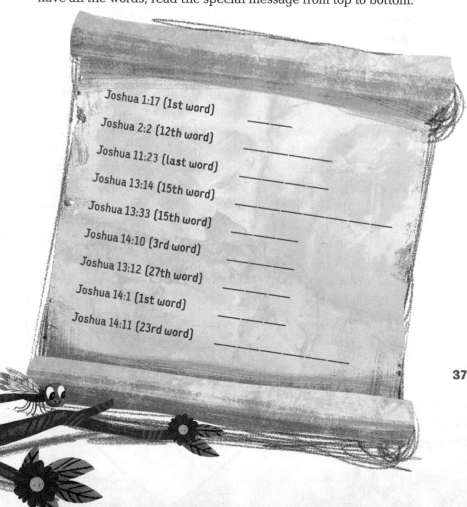

Find something true about God at the time of Joshua. It is also true for God's people today! Use the Bible verses to locate the words in the NIrV Bible. The number of blanks shows you how many letters the word has. When you have all the words, read the special message from top to bottom.

Joshua 1:17 (1st word)

Joshua 2:2 (12th word) ___ ___ ___

Joshua 11:23 (last word) ___ ___ ___ ___ ___

Joshua 13:14 (15th word) ___ ___ ___ ___ ___ ___

Joshua 13:33 (15th word) ___ ___ ___ ___ ___ ___ ___

Joshua 14:10 (3rd word) ___ ___ ___ ___

Joshua 13:12 (27th word) ___ ___ ___ ___

Joshua 14:1 (1st word) ___ ___ ___ ___ ___

Joshua 14:11 (23rd word) ___ ___ ___ ___ ___ ___ ___

Week 6, Day 3

Finding Jesus in Joshua

God was right there with the Israelites as they fought against their enemies. They had to trust that he would make sure they won the battle. When they did trust in God, Joshua led them to victory. God gave the Israelites peace and rest. Then they could enjoy the wonderful life God wanted them to have.

God does the same thing for us when we trust in Jesus! Joshua led the Israelites in their fight against their enemies. And Jesus leads us in our fight against sin. Jesus is right there with us as we fight against it. God tells us in the Bible that doing some things will hurt us. That's why those things are sin. Those things fight against us. Sometimes we might want to do those things anyway. But if we do, we won't have the peace and rest God wants for us. Jesus will help us win those battles over sin. All we have to do is trust in him. When we do, he will lead us to victory over sin. Then we will have peace and rest. We will be able to enjoy the wonderful life God wants us to have.

Jesus wants to bring us peace and rest. Write words or draw a picture to show how you feel when you think about Jesus.

38

Write About It

The Israelites had peace and rest after they won their battles. Jesus has won the battle against sin for us. Think about what that means for you. Write your thoughts here.

··

··

··

Joshua had to remind the Israelites to trust in God. That's because sometimes other things seemed stronger than God. What things do you sometimes think might be stronger than God? Write them here.

··

··

··

Week 6, Day 5

Pray About It

Dear God,

You gave the Israelites victory over their enemies. You gave them peace and rest. All these things happened when they trusted in you. Jesus won the battle over sin. He helps me to win the battle over sin too. Help me to trust him. Then I can have peace and rest. Thank you for being so good to me. I pray these things because I trust in Jesus.
Amen.

What do peace and rest mean to you? Draw or write about yourself being restful.

Do Something About It

Joshua and the Israelites were not as strong as the people they were trying to defeat. If they tried to win the battle on their own, they would lose every time. They needed God to give them the victory. They still had to do the fighting, but God made sure they won.

Use the boxes below to show Joshua and his army and those he was fighting. Draw something to show Joshua in one box and something to show the other army in the other box. What do you need to add to Joshua's box to make sure God's people win?

Now draw another set of boxes. Then draw something to show you in one box. Draw something to show a sin you are battling against in the other box. What do you need to add to your box to make sure you win your battle over that sin?

JOSHUA

Read About It

God raises up leaders to save the Israelites from the trouble their sin causes.

In the book of Judges, the Israelites were refusing to listen to God's instructions. That was causing big problems for them! God had given the Israelites the land he had promised them. They were living and raising their families in peace. There was so much for them to discover and enjoy. But they forgot all about God and how he had told them to live! God had told them how they could stay out of trouble. But they weren't listening to him anymore. So, guess what? They got into a lot of trouble. Their lives weren't good at all anymore!

Then the Israelites remembered God again. They asked God to save them from their trouble. Whenever they did this, God would bless them again. He would give a leader who would save the Israelites. Some of these leaders that God provided include Deborah, Gideon, and Samson. The Israelites could be happy again! In fact, they would get so happy that they would forget all about God again. Oh no! The Israelites were doing it all over again! They just kept repeating this pattern. Wouldn't they ever learn?

Think about something you did that you were told not to do. But then you did it anyway. Did bad things happen?

Think About It

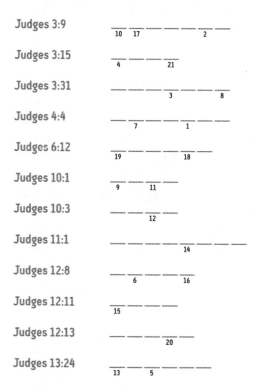

Use the Bible verses to find a secret message in the names of the Israelite leaders! Look up each verse in the NIrV. Write the name of the leader you find in that verse. The name will have the same number of letters as the blanks provided.

Judges 3:9   __ __ __ __ __ __ __
                  10 17   2

Judges 3:15   __ __ __ __
                4   21

Judges 3:31   __ __ __ __ __ __
                   3   8

Judges 4:4   __ __ __ __ __ __
                7   1

Judges 6:12   __ __ __ __ __ __
            19   18

Judges 10:1   __ __ __ __
            9   11

Judges 10:3   __ __ __ __
              12

Judges 11:1   __ __ __ __ __ __ __
                  14

Judges 12:8   __ __ __ __ __
            6   16

Judges 12:11   __ __ __ __
          15

Judges 12:13   __ __ __ __
             20

Judges 13:24   __ __ __ __ __ __
         13   5

43

Now write the numbered letters from above in the blanks below that have the same number.

__ __ __ __ __ __ __ __   __ __   __ __ __ __ __ __   __ __   __ __ __
1 2 3 4 5 6 7 8   9 10   11 12 13 14 15 16   17 18   19 20 21

Week 7, Day 3

Finding Jesus in Judges

You might think that we would never forget God like the Israelites did. But, we do! We act a lot like the Israelites do in Judges. Sometimes we don't listen to what he says. We act like we know better than God! And that kind of thinking gets us into all kinds of problems.

That's how the Israelites in the book of Judges got into all kinds of problems. But when they prayed to God, he gave them leaders who could save them. And God has given us a leader to save us. Our leader is Jesus! But Jesus is so much better than any of the leaders the Israelites had. Jesus is perfect! So, when he saves us, he does it perfectly. The Israelite leaders could only save them for a while. But Jesus saves us forever! All we must do is ask him for help. Jesus saves us from the punishment our sins deserve. We never need to worry about that again! And he does something else too. He shows us how to stay out of trouble. He shows us how to have the wonderful life God wants for us. We may still have trouble sometimes. But we should remember to ask Jesus for help!

Think about Jesus and about some other leaders in your own life. What things do you think make a great leader?

Week 7, Day 4

Write About It

Sometimes we get so busy that we even forget God! When the Israelites forgot God, they got into a lot of trouble. When we forget God, we can get into trouble too. Think of ways you can remember God and what he has told you in the Bible. Write your ideas here.

....

....

....

The Israelite leaders saved them from the trouble they got into. When we trust in Jesus, he saves us from worse trouble! He saves us from sin and all the harm it causes. Think about all the danger and harm Jesus has saved you from. How does that make you feel? Choose a color from Hearty's color chart. Then explain why you chose that color.

....

....

....

JUDGES

Pray About It

Dear God,

Thank you that Jesus has saved me from all the harm that sin causes. You want what is best for me. So please help me listen to you. Then sin can't hurt me. Sometimes I forget what you have said and get into trouble. When that happens, I know that I can ask Jesus for help. Thank you that he is always there for me. I pray these things because I believe in Jesus.

Amen.

Inside the giant T, write some of the times you've been in trouble. Complete the T to create a cross. Jesus can take your trouble away.

Do Something About It

You learned how much trouble the Israelites had when they didn't listen to God. If only they would have listened to him! Then their lives would have been so much better! Here is a way for you to remind yourself to listen to God. Get some crayons or markers. Have someone put a blindfold over your eyes. Make sure you can't see anything. Then have that person guide you as you color in the word below. Tell them not to let you color outside the lines. You'll have to listen to them carefully! No peeking!

Now tell the person that you don't want their help. You're not going to listen to them anymore. Keep the blindfold on. Try to color in the word below on your own this time. Again, no peeking!

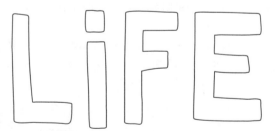

How did it go? How do you think doing this activity can be like listening or not listening to God?

Week 8, Day 1

Read About It

God makes empty lives full.

Do you know anyone who has lost almost everything? Well, Naomi was an Israelite woman who had lost almost everything she loved. While she was living in another country, her husband and two sons died. One daughter-in-law left her. All Naomi had left was her daughter-in-law, Ruth. These two women had no one to provide for them. They were lonely, scared, and hungry! Then Naomi decided to go back to Israel, her home country. And Ruth went along with her.

Naomi and Ruth thought their lives were so empty! But God is always faithful and loving. When they got to Israel, their empty life began to change. Ruth found a field where she could gather wheat. Now the women had some food to eat. The field belonged to a man named Boaz. Boaz was very kind. He decided to help them. He provided food for them. He also married Ruth. A while later, Boaz and Ruth had a baby boy named Obed. Obed would become the grandfather of King David. One day Jesus would be born from the family line of David. Wow! That is very important! Naomi had lost everything and thought her life was so empty. But God filled it with love and blessings again!

Naomi left Israel and moved to Moab for a better life. But things didn't turn out well. Find Moab on a map. Use the scale to learn how far away it was from Israel.

RUTH

Week 8, Day 2
Think About It

Read each sentence. Then read the Bible verses given
at the end of the sentence. The missing word is in the
verses and is also in the list below. You will use each
word in the list only once. But there are two words you won't use at all.

1. Boaz was from the town of _____ . (Read Ruth 2:4.)
2. Boaz was a _____ from Naomi's husband's family.
   (Read Ruth 2:1.)
3. Boaz also said to Ruth, "May the LORD, the God of Israel,
   _____ you richly. You have come to him to find
   _____ under his _____ ." (Read Ruth 2:12.)
4. Naomi told Ruth that Boaz is their _____ _____ .
   (Read Ruth 2:20.)
5. But Boaz told Ruth that there is someone more closely
   _____ to her than he is. (Read Ruth 3:12.)
6. Boaz agreed to _____ her if the other man does not.
   (Read Ruth 3:13.)
7. Boaz brought together the _____ of the town. (Read
   Ruth 4:2.)
8. The man said that he wouldn't buy Naomi's property. Then
   the man took off his _____ and gave it to Boaz. That
   showed the sale was final. (Read Ruth 4:7 and 8.)
9. Boaz spoke to the elders and all the people. He told them that
   he had bought all the _____ that belonged to Elimelek.
   And he said that he had taken Ruth to be his _____ .
   (Read Ruth 4:9 and 10.)

49

sandal	care	help	relative	baby
bitter	property	wife	elders	family
Bethlehem	bless	safety	related	protector

Finding Jesus in Ruth

In the book of Ruth, Boaz reminds us of Jesus. Boaz was a relative of Naomi and Ruth. He promised to take care of them. He saved and protected them. Jesus became a human being so that he could be our relative! Now when we believe in Jesus we know that he will save and protect us!

Who is a relative or someone like a relative who takes care of you?

Boaz was the great-grandfather of David. And Jesus would be born in the family line of David. God used Boaz not only to provide for Naomi and Ruth. God also used Boaz to provide the one who would provide for us! When we believe in Jesus, our empty lives can be full again!

Look at the scattered names below. These are the names of some of Jesus' family. Use what you already know about the Bible and the information in the book of Ruth. Put the names of the members of Jesus' family line in order using the lines.

Boaz	1. _____
Abraham	2. _____
Jesse	3. _____
David	4. _____
Isaac	5. _____
Mary	6. _____

50

Write About It

Some very bad things happened to Naomi. Her life seemed empty to her. Sometimes bad things happen to you. You might feel like your life is empty too. Write about a time you felt like that.

....

....

....

God cares about you! He wants your life to be full. God made sure Boaz was there to help Naomi and Ruth. God makes sure Jesus is there to help you! And when you believe in Jesus, he will provide the best life possible for you. Write inside the heart how that makes you feel.

Week 8, Day 5

Pray About It

Dear God,

I know you love me so much. Thank you for caring for your people in the past. You made their empty lives full with your blessings. Thank you for sending Jesus to help me. I know he will always protect and care for me. He keeps my life from being empty because he fills me with your blessings. Please help me to remember that you want me to have the best life possible! I pray these things because I believe in Jesus.

Amen.

How do you know God loves you? Write one reason in each heart.

Do Something About It

God wants you to remember his promise. When you believe in Jesus, you will never be alone. He is always with you to fill you with his blessings.

Here is an exploration that will help you remember God's promise to fill you with his blessings. Do this activity by a sink or over a bowl.

1. Take a paper or foam cup and fill it with the water.
2. Take a pin or thin nail and poke a hole in the bottom of the cup.
3. Watch the water drain out of the cup.
4. Then fill the cup with water again.
5. Watch the water drain out of the cup.
6. You can do this over and over again. You know the water will always drain out.

How does this remind you of God's promise to fill you with blessings? Let's think about it!

- The cup is like your life.
- The water is like God's blessings in your life.
- The nail hole or pin hole is like all the stuff that happens in your life. The stuff that takes you away from God and his blessings makes you feel empty inside.
- Write "I believe in Jesus" on a piece of tape and put the tape over the hole in the cup. Now fill the cup with water. None of the water drains out. When you believe in Jesus, your life will stay full of God's blessing. It will stay full just like the cup stayed full of water.

53

Week 9, Day 1

Read About It

God gives honor to humble people but he makes proud people humble.

Did you ever think that something was good only to find out it was bad? Maybe you bit into an apple and found a worm inside! Yuck! In 1 & 2 Samuel, the Israelites thought it would be good to have a king like all the other nations had. They had to learn for themselves that what they thought would be good could really be bad!

The kings of other nations depended on their own wisdom and strength. They were proud. But the king of Israel was not supposed to be like those kings! The kings of Israel were supposed to depend on the wisdom and strength of God. They were supposed to be humble. Saul was the first king of Israel. But Saul became like the kings of other nations. He became proud of himself and his authority. So, God made Saul humble by choosing someone else to be king!

God chose David to be the next king of his people. David was humble and depended on God. So, God gave David great honor. Sometimes David disobeyed God. But when he did, David admitted he had sinned and he returned to God. So, God promised to provide a king from David's family line. God said that this king would rule forever!

David did wrong things but later told the truth about them. Can you think of a time when you did something wrong? You either lied or disobeyed? What happened after that?

Week 9, Day 2

Think About It

David wrote a song of praise to God near the end of 1 & 2 Samuel. In this song David says something very important about proud people and humble people. Use the code below to figure out what the verse says. Find the letters for each word in the top row of the code. Then replace them with the letters under them. When you're done, you will be able to read the verse.

The Code

a	b	c	d	e	f	g	h	i	j	k	l	m	n	o	p	q	r	s	t	u	v	w	x	y	z
z	y	x	w	v	u	t	s	r	q	p	o	n	m	l	k	j	i	h	g	f	e	d	c	b	a

The Verse

___ ___ ___   ___ ___ ___ ___   ___ ___ ___ ___ ___   ___ ___ ___   ___ ___ ___   ___ ___ '
b l f   h z e v   g s l h v   d s l   z i v   m g

___ ___ ___ ___ ___   ___ ___ ___   ___ ___ ___   ___ ___ ___ ___ ___   ___ ___ ___
k i l f w   y f g   b l f   d z g x s   g s v

___ ___ ___ ___ ___   ___ ___   ___ ___ ___ ___ ___   ___ ___ ___ ___   ___ ___ ___ ___
k i l f w   g l   y i r m t   g s v n   w l d m

Week 9, Day 3

Finding Jesus in 1 & 2 Samuel

God promised King David that in the future he would provide another king from David's family line. And God said that this king would rule forever! God kept his promise to David. Many, many years later God brought this king into the world. And it was Jesus!

Jesus is perfect so he does perfectly what the Israelite kings couldn't always do. Jesus lived a humble life in every way. He always did what God the Father wanted him to do. That even included giving up his own life to save us. Isn't that wonderful! Jesus didn't even value his own life more than ours! Now that's being humble!

Below you see Jesus' name with five lines coming out of it. On each line write one word that has same meaning as the word "humble." Use a dictionary or thesaurus, or ask an adult for help. Think about what you know about Jesus. What did he do that showed he lives a humble life?

J ....

E ....

S ....

U ....

S ....

56

Write About It

David was a humble shepherd. He knew it was important to obey God's commands. He trusted that God would be with him all the time. So, when David faced the giant Goliath, he was not afraid. He knew God would be with him. You can trust that God will be with you, too, when you face scary things. Write how that makes you feel.

....

....

....

....

God wants you to be humble as you live your life. When you believe in Jesus, his Holy Spirit helps you to be humble. Write how that makes you feel.

....

....

....

....

Pray About It

Dear heavenly Father,
*   You have always loved your people. You want them to love and trust you. You want them to be humble. Please help me to be humble. You deserve all my praise and thanks for the gifts you have given me. Never let me become proud of myself and forget about you. I will praise you when I have success. And I will praise you when things don't go well for me. No matter what happens, I will honor and praise you. I pray this because I believe in Jesus. Amen.*

Think of some specific ways you can be humble in your everyday life. Write them on the notebook below. Use the list of words you brainstormed on Day 3.

Do Something About It

It's time to do some art! You'll need crayons or markers, and a sheet of 8 ½ x 11 or larger paper. Write HONOR GOD in the middle of the paper.

Using the crayons or markers write words in every direction around this sentence that remind you to praise and honor God. Here are some ideas to help you think of words to write.

- All the things you do that make you happy
- All the things you feel good about
- All the things you are good at doing

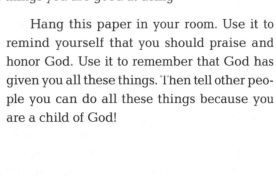

Hang this paper in your room. Use it to remind yourself that you should praise and honor God. Use it to remember that God has given you all these things. Then tell other people you can do all these things because you are a child of God!

1 & 2 KINGS

Read About It

God turns away from his people when their leaders turn away from him.

Have you ever lost a friend? Maybe you had an argument with them. Or maybe they just decided they didn't want to be your friend anymore. It probably was very hard for you! The same thing happened in 1 & 2 Kings. God's people decided they didn't want to be God's friends anymore!

It all started when King David chose his son Solomon to be king after him. At first Solomon was a wise and good king. But soon Solomon chose to worship false gods. So, after Solomon's death, God divided his kingdom into two nations. The northern kingdom was called Israel. The southern kingdom was called Judah. Both Israel and Judah chose to follow a path that would be bad for them. They chose to be unfaithful to God. Some prophets tried to get them to be God's friends again. But God's people turned away from him and from the life he wanted for them. God had no choice but to punish them for their sin. He allowed the Assyrians and the Babylonians to take his people away from their land. Israel and Judah were taken away from God's presence. It's a very sad story!

Why do you think God's people didn't want to be his friends anymore? Why didn't they listen to the warnings of God's prophets? Why did they think this would be okay? Didn't they know this would be bad for them?

....
....
....
....
....
....
....
....
....
....
....
....
....
....
....

61

Think About It

Read the Bible verses beside each king's name. Those verses will tell you whether the king was good or bad. Write "good" or "bad" in the blank before each name. If the king followed God, look for his name in the Good Kings word search. If the king didn't follow God, look for his name in the Bad Kings word search. The names in the word search go forward, backward, up, down, or at an angle.

_____ JEROBOAM   1 Kings 13:33

_____ ABIJAH   1 Kings 15:3

_____ ASA   1 Kings 15:9–11

_____ NADAB   1 Kings 15:25–26

_____ OMRI   1 Kings 16:25

_____ AHAB   1 Kings 16:30

_____ JEHOSHAPHAT   1 Kings 22:42–43

_____ MENAHEM   2 Kings 15:17–18

_____ JOTHAM   2 Kings 15:32–34

_____ AHAZ   2 Kings 16:1–2

_____ HEZEKIAH   2 Kings 18:1–3

_____ MANASSEH   2 Kings 21:1–2

_____ JOSIAH   2 Kings 22:1–2

_____ JEHOIAKIM   2 Kings 23:36–37

_____ ZEDEKIAH   2 Kings 24:18–19

GOOD KINGS

H	A	I	K	Є	Z	Є	H	M	V	L	C	H	K	N
H	G	J	X	X	K	A	S	D	A	Y	X	A	Y	B
N	N	H	S	P	A	A	R	L	I	H	T	I	Є	W
J	Є	H	O	S	H	A	P	H	A	T	T	S	G	K
G	W	X	A	Z	B	Z	D	M	B	X	A	O	J	Z
L	R	T	Y	J	S	M	U	D	P	M	W	J	J	X
P	S	S	Z	Q	X	K	J	Q	X	T	M	Z	A	D

BAD KINGS

J	Є	H	O	I	A	K	I	M	Є	N	A	H	Є	M
B	A	H	A	Z	J	M	F	F	H	A	J	I	B	A
H	A	I	K	Є	D	Є	Z	F	B	C	C	V	Z	G
I	M	D	C	Y	K	F	M	A	N	A	S	S	Є	H
R	O	Z	A	D	R	R	H	L	W	K	S	V	J	M
M	G	Є	S	N	M	A	O	B	O	R	Є	J	L	L
O	M	H	J	Y	K	M	Є	W	Є	V	D	A	W	O

63

Finding Jesus in 1 & 2 Kings

1 & 2 KINGS

Sometimes we do the same things the bad kings of Israel did. Doing those things is like saying we don't want to be friends with God anymore! We keep ourselves from having the best life God wants for us.

God wants so much for us to have the best life possible. So, he sent his son Jesus to be our good king. Jesus never turned away from God like we sometimes do. And Jesus paid the price for all the times we do turn away from God. That's why when Jesus was on the cross, God had to let him suffer! Can you imagine how much that must have hurt Jesus? But because Jesus did that for us, we don't have to worry. God will never turn away from anyone who believes in Jesus!

Decorate a crown fit for our good king, Jesus.

Write About It

Suppose you don't listen to your parents or teachers and you do whatever you want. Then you get into trouble. That's a lot like what happened to Israel and Judah when they turned away from God. Write here how you feel when you don't listen and get into trouble.

....

....

....

Sometimes you don't listen to God and do what you want to do. That's sneaky sin's way of turning you away from God. When you ask God to forgive you, he will do it. God loves you that much! He sent Jesus to take away all your sins. When you believe in Jesus, your sins are forgiven. Write how knowing that makes you feel. Choose a color from Hearty's color chart and tell about it.

....

....

....

65

Week 10, Day 5

Pray About It

Thank you, dear God, for loving me so much. Thank you for sending your son Jesus. He paid the price for my turning away from you. Help me not to turn away from you anymore. Help me to make choices that will keep me close to you. Help me to love you and do what you want me to do. I ask this because I believe in Jesus.
Amen.

Cut out or make your own copy of this sign. Hang your sign.

1. Stop
2. Think of God.
3. Make a good choice.

Do Something About It

When we believe in Jesus, we don't want to turn away from God. Let's try something that will help you remember this. Find two flat magnets. Try putting them together.

When you put one side of the magnets together, the magnets stick tightly. That's like the times you choose to follow God's commands. You're choosing to stick tightly to him! Now turn the magnets around. When you try to put the magnets together now, they don't stick. In fact, they might even push away from each other! That's like the times you choose to follow your own way instead of doing what God has said!

Make a list of eight things you can do that will keep you sticking tightly to God. Start your list below, then copy it on a card or piece of paper. Use a magnet to put the card or paper on your refrigerator.

Things I can do to keep me sticking tightly to God:

1. _____

2. _____

3. _____

4. _____

5. _____

6. _____

7. _____

8. _____

67

1 & 2 CHRONICLES

Week 11, Day 1

Read About It

God encourages the Israelites by reminding them of his promises to their faithful kings.

Have you ever heard of Eshtemoa? Or how about Mishma? These names might sound strange to you. They're just a couple names from 1 and 2 Chronicles, a book full of names! But these names reminded the Israelites that God had been with his people since the beginning. So they could be sure that he would be with them in the future too!

The Israelites needed to be reminded of this. Things had gone badly for them because they turned away from God. So, God sent them away from the land he had given them. Now Cyrus the Persian king had let them come back to their land. But they wondered if God still loved them. They needed to be encouraged! 1 and 2 Chronicles do this by reminding the Israelites of the faithful kings they had in the past. David and Solomon were the best kings. They listened to God and followed his instructions. So God made wonderful promises to those kings. He had promised to bless them in the future. God would bless the Israelites too because of them. God promised David and Solomon that rulers would be born to them. And God would love them forever. So, the Israelites had a reason to hope for good things in the future!

Do you ever need to be encouraged? What makes you happier when you are sad?

Week 11, Day 2

Think About It

Look at the key. Write the letter for each object using the key. Then read the sentence that results. It will remind you of the main idea of Chronicles.

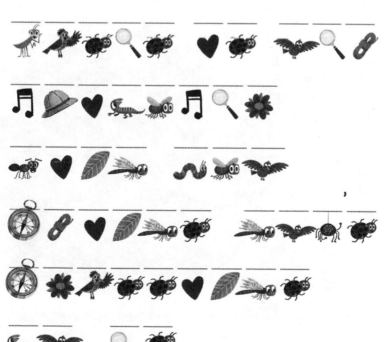

69

Week 11, Day 3

Finding Jesus in
1 & 2 Chronicles

1 and 2 Chronicles encouraged the Israelites by reminding them of David and Solomon. God made promises to those faithful kings. And all those promises applied to all the people in their kingdom. God made those promises to David and Solomon because they tried to be faithful to God. But even these good kings were not perfect. Even they disobeyed God at times. But God promised them there would be another king born in their family line. He would be a king who would come in the future. And he would always be perfectly faithful to God. He would always follow God's instructions. So God would bless that king with a kingdom that would last forever.

That new king is Jesus! He rules right now from heaven. And one day he will return to rule forever on earth.

When we believe in Jesus, we can be encouraged too. How does knowing that Jesus is our perfect king make you feel? Write your feelings on the branches of the tree.

Write About It

1 & 2 CHRONICLES

In 1 and 2 Chronicles, we find many names of God's people in the past. God was faithful to all of them. That encouraged the Israelites who came back to the land God had given them. Think of people in your life who have trusted God. How does their faith encourage you? Write your thoughts here.

....

....

....

Jesus is perfectly faithful. We are not always faithful. But when we trust in Jesus, his faithfulness is counted as ours. We don't have to worry that we're not good enough for heaven. Jesus makes us good enough! How does that make you feel?

....

....

....

Week 11, Day 5

Pray About It

Thank you, God, for sending Jesus to be my king. He was perfectly faithful to you. So, he has earned all of the blessings you promised. And he gives those blessings to me! Please make me faithful like him. Help me follow your instructions. Then I will have the wonderful life you want me to have. I ask you for these things because I believe in Jesus.
Amen.

Color the verse below.

But be STRONG.
Don't give up.
God will
reward
YOU for your WORK.

-2 Chronicles 15:7

Do Something About It

God encourages us in our faith by reminding us about Jesus. Jesus makes sure our relationship with God lasts forever. That really helps when we're sad or don't think we're good enough for God. All we must do is remember Jesus is our king. Because of him, God will love us forever!

It feels good to be encouraged by God like this. We can encourage other people in the same way. Write the name of one person you could encourage by telling them about Jesus.

....

Make sure you talk to that person this week! They might want Jesus to be their king too.

Sometimes people who already believe in Jesus have a hard time. They might be like the Israelites in 1 and 2 Chronicles. Write the name of someone like that.

....

God will always love them! You could help them a lot by reminding them of God's love.

73

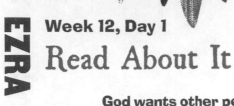

Week 12, Day 1

Read About It

God wants other people to be able to see our love for him.

God's people had been away from their own land for a long time! When they returned, they wanted to rebuild the temple. They knew that was an important thing to do. It would show other people how much they loved God.

After the temple was rebuilt, Ezra arrived. He was an important priest and teacher of God's people. Ezra told them that there was something even more important than the temple. The temple was only a building. God was more interested in people. God wanted his people to show how much they loved him. God wanted them to show this love by how they lived. Then other people would really see how much they loved God!

What are some things you could do to help people see that you love God?

Think About It

Find these important words from the book of Ezra.
Use the list of words by the puzzle.

EZRA

H	S	K	F	C	R	E	T	U	R	N	Y	C	H	D
X	S	B	C	P	V	I	F	A	T	D	I	G	O	E
X	E	R	X	E	S	H	S	E	L	I	X	E	R	D
E	F	I	A	N	V	C	S	J	N	U	Z	A	E	I
Z	N	F	S	Z	Q	A	R	E	J	L	T	S	Y	C
G	O	T	W	L	R	P	C	R	M	E	X	U	A	A
J	C	E	R	C	I	T	O	U	E	S	I	R	R	T
L	J	M	A	C	H	I	M	S	M	I	J	Y	P	E
U	X	P	T	E	K	V	M	A	O	M	T	C	Z	L
F	Y	L	L	I	F	E	Z	L	H	O	S	A	E	H
H	J	E	A	L	F	Z	Z	E	P	R	C	E	Z	A
T	L	D	A	R	I	U	S	M	J	P	E	R	R	D
I	I	S	R	R	G	P	K	D	U	T	H	R	A	U
A	R	W	Z	I	M	H	U	M	T	V	I	W	A	J
F	Q	N	H	S	E	Y	D	R	E	B	U	I	L	D

altar	Darius	faithful	prayer	temple
captive	dedicate	home	promise	Xerxes
confess	exiles	Jerusalem	rebuild	
Cyrus	Ezra	Judah	return	

EZRA

Finding Jesus in Ezra

When God's people returned to their land, they built the temple. The temple was the place where they could meet with God.

When Jesus came, he was called Immanuel. That means "God with us." Read Matthew 1:23. When people believe in Jesus, they can meet with God. And when they believe in Jesus, he makes *them* his temple! That's what the apostle Paul says in 1 Corinthians 3:16. In that verse, he asks believers, "Don't you know that you yourselves are God's temple?"

Everyone who believes in Jesus is part of the new temple of God! Ephesians 2:21 describes this new temple. Color in the words of this verse to see what it says about Jesus.

The whole building
is held together by him.
It rises to become a
holy temple
because it belongs to
the Lord.

—EPHESIANS 2:21

Write About It

The people in the book of Ezra set apart the new temple to God. This means that they promised to use the temple to worship and serve God. People who believe in Jesus are God's new temple. That means that we should worship and serve God too. When we do this, we show God how much we love him. Other people around us will see this too. How do you feel knowing God wants you to worship him?

....

....

....

....

Think about how people worship and serve God. What are some things you could do to show other people how much you love God? Describe four of them here.

....

....

....

....

EZRA

Pray About It

Dear God,

Thank you for making me part of your new temple! I want this temple to be something you are proud of. I want to show other people my love for you. Please help me to do this better.

Amen.

In the book of Ezra, the people had to be reminded that God lived with them. He didn't just live in the temple but in their hearts as well. They needed to show their love for God by how they lived. The titles on the boxes below suggest different ways you can do this. Write your ideas for showing your love for God in each of the boxes.

Speaking

Doing

Thinking

Do Something About It

This adventure will remind you how God is building his new temple. He is building it with those who believe in Jesus! So, believers have to be sure the temple shows people what Jesus is like.

Use building blocks, books, or other things that can be stacked to create a wall. Label the blocks with words that describe Jesus.

Use these six words and then add six of your own.

Forgiveness	Mercy	Peace
Kindness	Love	Goodness

```
                    KINDNESS

            GOODNESS    ..............

        MERCY   ..............    PEACE

   LOVE    ..............  FORGIVENESS   ..............
```

Week 13, Day 1

Read About It

God wants people who love him to be different than those who don't.

Nehemiah was in Persia serving the king. Then he heard something about Jerusalem that made him very sad. He heard that its walls were still broken down. This made it hard to tell who were God's people and who weren't.

So, Nehemiah went back to Jerusalem. He helped God's people rebuild the wall around the city. It was hot and sweaty work. And that wasn't the only hard part! The other people living around Jerusalem didn't want God's people to build the wall! They wanted God's people to be just like them! And many of God's people wanted to be just like those other people. After all, who wants to be different from everyone else? Would God's people be willing to turn away from God to be like everyone else?

Nehemiah encouraged God's people to be different! And God's people listened to him. God's people decided they would live the way God had told them to live. By doing that, they would be a blessing to the people living around them. They would show those people the new, better life God wanted for them. God's people could only do that if they were living differently than the people around them.

How does doing the right thing help people see what God is like? Can people see something true about God by looking at what you do?

Think About It

God wants people to be able to see the better life he wants for them. So, God's people have to live differently than those who don't know God. We do that by living as God has told us in the Bible. Then other people will be able to see the difference. We'll be showing them the better life God wants them to have too! Can people see that you live differently because you follow God? Can they spot the differences?

Let's see if *you* can spot the differences in the two drawings below. Thinky has a twin! Well, almost. Can you find at least five differences between the Thinky on the left and the Thinky on the right? Circle each one you find.

Finding Jesus in Nehemiah

Nehemiah obeyed God. He never strayed from his task of helping God's people obey God. He helped them do this even when other people didn't want them to!

In this way, he was predicting how Jesus would act. Jesus always obeyed the Father. He continually prayed to the Father for help to do this. Jesus would bring physical and spiritual healing. He would bring it to the people of Judah and all the people of the world. Everyone who believes in him can join with him in this work.

God wants all of us to be brave and faithful and to keep doing his work. He wants us to do this even when other people try to stop us. Make a plan for how you will help with Jesus' work on earth. Write your ideas below for how you can physically and spiritually help people.

Physical Help	Spiritual Help

Write About It

On day 2 of this week, you spotted the differences between the two pictures. Think about your own life. Do people see anything different about you because you believe in Jesus? Think about the things you do differently than people who don't know Jesus. Write a few of those things in the notebook.

Did you ever do something even though you know God said it was wrong? Think about why you did it. How did it keep other people from seeing the better life God wants for them? Write your thoughts here.

Week 13, Day 5

Pray About It

Dear God,

Thank you for telling me how to live the best possible life. Sometimes it is hard to do. Sometimes people want me to do things you've said are wrong. Those things can hurt me. But sometimes I do them anyway. Please forgive me and help me to live more like Jesus. Then my life will become more like the way you want it to be. And then I will be showing other people a better way to live too. I ask you for these things because I believe in Jesus.

Amen.

Just like the Jews rebuilt the wall of their city, we also need to lay down bricks to build our best life possible. In the blocks below, write six things that can help you live the best life possible.

Do Something About It

God's people started to be like the people who lived around them. Those people didn't believe in God! Nehemiah told God's people they had to be different. They had to show other people a better way to live. That's the way of life God had told them about.

Use the space below to write your plan for living the way God wants you to live. Your plan might include ways you will praise God or help other people. There are all sorts of things you can do! These things will show other people the better life God wants for them too.

It is important to follow up. After a few days, ask yourself how your plan is working out.

I will ask God to help me to

Week 14, Day 1

Read About It

God puts people in the right place to save his people from their enemies.

Have you ever talked to someone who didn't answer you? Maybe they didn't even hear or notice you. Maybe you had to say something like, "Hey, didn't you hear what I said?" Sometimes it might seem like God doesn't hear us or notice us. It might have seemed that way to Esther. Another nation had won the victory over God's people. Esther had been taken away to live in a land far away. She even had to serve the king of Persia! In fact, he had made her his queen. Esther was probably wondering why God was letting all this happen. Didn't he hear her prayers? But God was still at work, even though Esther couldn't see it.

God had put Esther and her cousin Mordecai in a special place for a special purpose. God would use them to save the lives of all God's people! The king that Esther served had a very mean official whose name was Haman. Haman hated God's people and secretly planned to kill them. But Mordecai found out about Haman's plan and told Esther about it. She was able to get the king to stop Haman's plan. And the only person who ended up getting killed was Haman! What Haman wanted to happen to God's people happened to him instead! God's people were safe! God had rescued them!

You probably like reading stories about people who are brave. Those people do what is right even when it's hard and scary. The book of Esther is one of those stories! Think about what you would do if you were her.

86

Think About It

ESTHER

God had a special purpose for Mordecai and Esther. God used them to save all his people from their enemies! When you solve this word puzzle, you will discover two things. You will discover the name God has given you. And you will discover the special purpose he has for you.

Solve this word puzzle. Notice that the letters under the blank lines don't make sense. You will have to discover what the words are. To do this you will have to use the letter in the alphabet just after the one given. For example, the first letter under the first blank line is B. The letter just after B is C. So, the first letter of the first word in the puzzle is C. The alphabet is given here to help you.

A B C D E F G H I J K L M N O P Q R S T U V W X Y Z

"You are C h __ __ __ __ ' __ __ __ __ __ __ __
        B G Q H R S R   N E E H B H Z K

__ __ __ __ __ __ __ __ __ __ ."
L D R R D M F D Q R

__ __ __ __   __ __ __ __ __   __ __ __ __ __ __   __ __ __ __ __
S D K K   N S G D Q   O D N O K D   Z A N T S

__ __ __ __ __ !
I D R T R

Week 14, Day 3

Finding Jesus in Esther

The situation for Esther, Mordecai, and all God's people looked hopeless. They had been taken to a land far away from the land God had given them. Now other people ruled over them. And they would all die unless someone provided a way to save them. God in his great mercy did that. God put Mordecai and Esther in the right place and at the right time. God used them to save his people from their enemies.

God has done the same thing for us! Sin is our enemy and wants to rule over us. In fact, it wants to kill us! And it will kill us unless someone provides a way to save us from it. And God in his great mercy did that! When the time was just right, God sent his Son, Jesus. Jesus came to earth. He lived, died, and rose again to rescue us from our sin.

When God saved his people in the book of Esther, Mordecai sent messengers to everyone to let them know. Now God also has a special purpose for us. He wants us to be his messengers to tell everyone about Jesus. We need to tell them how Jesus came to rescue us.

In the scroll below, write some ways that you can tell others about Jesus.

Write About It

God used Esther and Mordecai to save his people from their enemies. Then Mordecai sent out messengers to let everyone know about it! God sent his son Jesus to save his people from sin. And God wants you to let everyone know about it! Write how that makes you feel.

....

....

....

Esther was afraid to do what Mordecai asked her to do. At first, she didn't want to do it. She asked God's people to pray for her. God wants you to talk about his plan to save other people. He will save them when they believe in Jesus. But you might be scared to tell people the good news about Jesus. You can pray and ask God to help you do this. How could God help you tell other people about Jesus? Write your thoughts here.

....

....

....

Week 14, Day 5

Pray About It

Dear God,

You are a great and wonderful God. You love your people and rescue them from their enemies. Thank you for sending Jesus to rescue me. He won the victory over sin. I know you want me to tell other people about this. But sometimes I am afraid. Please help me to have courage to tell other people about Jesus. I ask this because I believe in Jesus.
Amen!

On the lines next to Talky, write what you would like to tell people about Jesus.

Do Something About It

God had put Esther in a special place where she could help her people when the time came. She was a queen but she still had to be very brave to save God's people.

Create a crown to remind you of queen Esther and her faithfulness to God. It will also remind you that God wants you to be strong in your faith too. You don't have to wear the crown. But hang it in your room as a reminder to be faithful to God like Queen Esther.

You will need construction paper, scissors, tape or a stapler, and decorating items. Create the shape of the front of the crown using construction paper. Decorate it. Then cut a 1-inch-wide strip of paper to create a headband and attach the front of the crown to it. See the drawings below for some creative ideas.

91

Week 15, Day 1

Read About It

God sometimes does things that we can't understand.

Don't you wonder why God does some things? It's especially hard for us to understand when bad things happen to us or other people. We might think, "How could God let this happen?" The book of Job is one way God answers this question for us.

When the book begins, Job has a great life. But is Job happy because he has a good family and lots of stuff? Or is he happy because he is a child of God? Satan thinks it's because Job has a great family and lots of stuff. So, God lets Satan take away all the possessions Job has. That makes Job very sad.

Job's friends show up to make him feel better. But they only make things worse! They tell Job he must have done something wrong. But Job knows that is not true. So why *is* God letting these bad things happen to him? God told Job that there are many things he can see and know that Job can't. For example, Job didn't know that God was showing Job's faith to Satan. That's why all those terrible things happened to him. God told Job that human beings can't know things like God does. But there is one thing we can always be sure of. And that is that God loves us!

Think about a time when something bad happened to you that you feel you didn't deserve. How did you feel? How did other people feel?

Think About It

God reminds Job that Job can only see a small part of what's going on. Only God can see the whole picture. From our point of view, things may not make sense. But from God's bigger point of view they do make sense! We see the small picture. God sees the big picture! This fun activity will remind you of this. You can see five small pictures below. Each picture shows a small part of something much bigger. You might not be able to tell what the bigger thing is. That's because you can only see these smaller parts of them. See if you can guess what the bigger thing is! Write the name of the item on the line.

1. _____ 2. _____ 3. _____

4. _____ 5. _____

Week 15, Day 3

Finding Jesus in Job

Job couldn't figure out why all sorts of bad things were happening to him. He couldn't see the bigger picture that only God could see. Job's friends told him that the bad things were happening because Job had done something wrong. But that wasn't true. Bad things can happen to a person who hasn't done anything wrong at all. That's what happened to Jesus!

Certainly, Jesus never did anything wrong! But all sorts of bad things happened to him! So, bad things really can happen to good people. Only God knows the reason why bad things happen. Sometimes he lets us know that reason. God tells us why bad things happened to Jesus. They happened to him because he was paying the price for our sins. And because Jesus paid the price for our sins, God can forgive us! When we trust in Jesus, we can be God's children!

Reading the story of Job helps us remember that bad things can happen to good people. We won't always understand why. But because we belong to Jesus, we can talk to Jesus about them!

What are some bad things that have happened to you? List them beside the praying hands. Then tell Jesus about them.

94

Write About It

Has a parent or teacher ever encouraged you do something you really didn't like to do? Maybe you had to study for a test. Maybe they made you eat your vegetables. Maybe they wanted you to be nice to your brother or sister. How could they do that! Write how that made you feel.

....

....

....

Think of the good reasons why your parent or teacher suggested you do those things. Write your thoughts here.

....

....

....

Pray About It

Dear God,

Sometimes I get angry when things don't go my way. But I know that I can't see the big picture like you can. You know everything. But I do know that you have made me your child and love me! I know that you love me whether bad things or good things happen. Help me to trust you even when bad things happen. I ask you for this because I believe in Jesus. Amen.

Have you ever said the three words "It's not fair"? Lots of kids do. It's hard to always understand the reasons things happen to us. But we should trust that God is taking care of us. And that's true whether what is happening is good or bad. For each letter in the words below, think of a positive word. Then explain why you chose that word. The first one is done for you.

I   Important. What God is doing is important.

T' _____

S _____

N _____

O _____

T _____

F _____

A _____

I _____

R! _____

Week 15, Day 6

Do Something About it

Sometimes it's hard to understand why God does certain things. God's reasons are often things we would never think of. Here is a fun way to think about why things happen. Use the words in the lists below. You and a friend take turns filling in the blanks for this sentence. "I bought a __A__ so that I could __B__." The first person must use the first words in columns A and B. You might end up with a pretty silly sentence! Now the second person must use the second words in the columns. Keep taking turns until you've used up all the words. Have fun thinking of interesting ways the words can go together. Be creative!

When you're done going through the lists in order, switch things around. Try starting with the first word in one list and the last word in the other list.

A	B
horse	go to school
pizza	stay up late
video game	take a day off school
puppy	go swimming
computer	get home on time
chocolate bar	play with my friends
gift for my mom	eat ice cream
a ball cap	watch TV
backpack	read a book
soda	go to the store

97

Week 16, Day 1

Read About It

God wants us to talk with him no matter how we feel.

Do you have a best friend? If you do, you may love to explore together. You probably spend a lot of time talking to each other. You like to share your thoughts and ideas. Best friends trust each other too. That's the kind of relationship God wants with his people!

God wants his people to spend time with him. God wants them to trust him. He wants them to share their thoughts, ideas, and feelings with him. That's true whether things are good or bad. And God even wants his people to share their biggest secrets with him! That's the kind of relationship God wants with his people.

Psalms are one way God's people in the Old Testament talked with him. God's people today can use these same words. They can be used by anyone when they talk with God. The psalms teach us about who God is and what he has done. They also help us talk to God about our deepest feelings and emotions. And we can do that when we're happy, when we're sad, or even when we're angry. Psalms help God's people talk with him no matter how they're feeling! Like a best friend, God just wants to hear from us!

What are some of the things you talk to God about? Do you feel better after you talk to him?

Week 16, Day 2

Think About It

The psalms give us ways to tell God how we feel.
Each verse below talks about a feeling. Read the
verses and then fill in the missing word in the verse.
Notice the number under each letter of the word. Write those letters
in the box with the same number in the puzzle. When you're done
with this adventure, you'll have a poem about this book of poems!

1. **Psalm 3:6** I won't be ___ ___ ___ ___ ___ ___ even though tens of
   $\quad$ $\quad$ $\quad$ $\quad$ $\quad$ 1 $\;$ 2 $\;$ 3 $\;$ 4 $\;$ 5 $\;$ 6

   thousands attack me on every side.

2. **Psalm 6:3** My soul is very ___ ___ ___ ___ ___ ___ ___ ___.
   $\quad$ $\quad$ $\quad$ $\quad$ 7 $\;$ 8 $\;$ 9 $\;$ 10 $\;$ 11 $\;$ 12 $\;$ 13 $\;$ 14

3. **Psalm 16:6** I am very ___ ___ ___ ___ ___ with what I've received
   $\quad$ $\quad$ $\quad$ 15 $\;$ 16 $\;$ 17 $\;$ 18 $\;$ 19

   from you.

4. **Psalm 30:11** You removed my clothes of ___ ___ ___ ___ ___ ___ ___ and
   $\quad$ $\quad$ $\quad$ 20 $\;$ 21 $\;$ 22 $\;$ 23 $\;$ 24 $\;$ 25 $\;$ 26

   dressed me with ___ ___ ___.
   $\quad$ $\quad$ 27 $\;$ 28 $\;$ 29

5. **Psalm 32:11** Be ___ ___ ___ ___ because of what the Lord has done
   $\quad$ $\quad$ 30 $\;$ 31 $\;$ 32 $\;$ 33

   for you.

6. **Psalm 38:8** I am ___ ___ ___ ___. I feel as if I've been broken in
   $\quad$ $\quad$ 34 $\;$ 35 $\;$ 36 $\;$ 37

   pieces.

5	2		29	9	10		2	13	24	31		20	7	3	28	23	30
	28	8		34	13	1	37										
7	9		30	28	6												
19	28	10		25	15	28	10	31	6		25	17	35	16	37		

Week 16, Day 3

Finding Jesus in Psalms

The book of Psalms tells us about God. This book shows us it's okay for God's people to talk with him about anything. In other words, Psalms shows us what a healthy relationship with God looks like. Jesus shows us all those things too!

Some psalms talk about God as king. James 5:4 says that Jesus rules over all. Some psalms talk about God forgiving sin. Jesus forgives sin in Matthew 9:2. Some psalms talk about God's kindness and tender care for his people. In the New Testament, we read about the kindness and tender care of Jesus too. Many psalms talk about God's love. Here is what Jesus says in John 15:13. "No one has greater love than the one who gives their life for their friends." And that's exactly what Jesus has done for us!

Look up the verses below. Draw a line to match the Psalm to the verse in the New Testament that best matches its message.

Psalm 34:18   Matthew 9:2

Psalm 65:3   John 15:13

Psalm 36:7   Luke 1:78–79

Week 16, Day 4

Write About It

Talking with God is so important for your relationship with him! You can tell God anything. He really wants to hear from you! Write how that makes you feel.

....

....

....

Here's what the Bible says in Philippians 4:6–7. "Don't worry about anything. No matter what happens, tell God about everything. Ask and pray, and give thanks to him. Then God's peace will watch over your hearts and your minds. He will do this because you belong to Christ Jesus." Write how this makes you feel.

....

....

....

Week 16, Day 5

Pray About It

Dear God,

Thank you for loving me so much. I know you want to hear from me when I am happy or sad or hurt! Please help me be willing to tell you how I feel. Thank you for being ready to listen to me at any time. Help me to spend more time talking with you in prayer. Thank you for giving me the psalms to show me how to do this. I pray this because I believe in Jesus. Amen!

Color the verse below. Think about the words as you color them.

I LOOK UP TO THE MOUNTAINS.
WHERE DOES MY HELP COME FROM?
MY HELP COMES FROM
the LORD.
HE IS THE MAKER OF
heaven and earth.

—PSALM 121:1-2

Do Something About It

The Psalms are poems. They are like some poems because they talk about feelings and emotions. But the Psalms are different from other poems because all the Psalms focus on God. They tell us who God is and what he does. They also tell God who we are and how we're feeling. Many different people wrote the Psalms. They all talked about their emotions and feelings with God.

Now it's your turn to write your own psalm. Begin by deciding what emotion or feeling you want to talk to God about. Think about how you will say it. Write that on the first line. Then think about what God has done for you. Write about that on the second line. Remember, it doesn't have to rhyme. It just has to be honest! This is only the beginning. Write as many lines as you want. God wants to hear from you! When you're done writing your psalm, put it away someplace safe. It is a private talk between you and God.

Week 17, Day 1

Read About It

God tells us how to live according to the order he has built into his creation.

Think of wisdom as a person. Here is what Proverbs 8:32–34 tells us that person would say to us: "My children, listen to me. Blessed are those who keep my ways. Listen to my teaching and be wise. Don't turn away from it. Blessed are those who listen to me."

The wisdom of Proverbs tells us how God made the world work. It tells us about the order that God has built into his creation. It tells us how we can live according to that order. Living that way is what Proverbs calls wise. Making wise choices results in things going so much better for us! We learn how to live in God's world. We learn how to live well with each other. And we learn how to live as God's children. God provided someone to show us what it looks like to live this way. God sent his own son, Jesus, to show us how to live wisely.

Who do you think is wise? What makes them seem wise to you?

Think About It

Proverbs tells us that God holds the world together. But in this puzzle, the world has gone to pieces! Can you put it back together? Cut out these 16 pieces. Arrange the pieces so that the world is right again.

PROVERBS

Finding Jesus in Proverbs

Jesus shows us what it looks like to live wisely. He shows us that it means living with respect for God. That means we'll try to grow in our relationship with him. We'll read the Bible and try to live as he has instructed us. Jesus also shows us that living wisely means living with respect for ourselves. God thinks we're special, so we should treat ourselves that way too. We should never do anything to hurt ourselves. And Jesus shows us that living wisely also means respecting the rest of God's creation. God made everything. So when we treat his creation with respect, we're treating God with respect!

Jesus shows us so much about God's wisdom that he is even called wisdom! Here is what the apostle Paul says about Jesus in 1 Corinthians 1:30. "He has become God's wisdom for us." So, becoming wise is the same thing as becoming like Jesus!

Rate your wisdom. Choose a number on the scale below that shows how wise you think you are.

Then write some ideas of how you can become wiser like Jesus.

0 1 2 3 4 5 6 7 8 9 10

Write About It

Sometimes we do things without really thinking. This can lead to big problems! What if you rode your bike without paying attention to where you were going? Yikes! Take some time to think about the things you do. Why do you do them? Write your thoughts here.

....

....

....

God tells us the best way to live. But sometimes people try to get us not to follow God's directions. They might even call us names or make life difficult. What do you do when that happens? How does that make you feel?

....

....

....

PROVERBS

Pray About It

Dear God,

Thank you for creating such a wonderful world! Thank you for creating me. Please help me to learn to live wisely in your wonderful world. Thank you for sending your own Son, Jesus, to show me what that looks like. Help me to understand what he is showing me with his life. I want to live my life wisely as Jesus did. I know that when I do, I'll be living just as you created me to live. Then other people can see the life that you want for them too. I ask you for these things because I believe in Jesus.
Amen.

The book of Proverbs tells us how to live wisely. Here are some proverbs that describe what it means to live wisely. Look them up and write them down so you can remember them.

Write out Proverbs 6:6—It talks about working hard.

....

Write out Proverbs 16:20—It talks about the kind of person God blesses.

....

Write out Proverbs 17:17—It talks about being a friend.

....

Write out Proverbs 22:24—It talks about the danger of hanging around with angry people.

....

Do Something About It

Most of the time we can't see the order God has placed in the world. So sometimes we forget that God is holding things together. We forget that he has made the world work the way it does. Here is an exploration that will remind you that God has put things together. You can do that by taking apart something in nature.

You can take apart light! Here's a simple way to do it.

You'll need a clear drinking glass and a sheet of white paper. Sometimes this works better if the glass has straight sides. Fill the glass a little over halfway with water. Go outside or near a window where the sun is shining. Hold the glass of water above the paper. The sunlight will divide into all the colors of the rainbow! You might need to move the glass of water around a bit to see it. You are separating the sunlight into all its different colors. This happens when the sunlight passes through the water. It's the same thing that happens when you see a rainbow in the sky! You don't always see all the different colors because they combine to form sunlight. God holds them all together.

Draw boxes below showing the colors you saw.

Week 18, Day 1

Read About It

God leads us to think about the purpose of life.

Suppose you had $20.00. How would you spend it? You'd want to spend it on something good, right? You'd want it to be worth your $20.00! If you think about it, you have a life to spend too. What are you going to spend it on? You want it to be worth it, right? The person who wrote the book of Ecclesiastes thought about that a lot. He is called the Teacher. The Teacher was so important and had so much money that he could do anything he wanted. So how should he spend his life?

The Teacher thought maybe life was all about learning a lot of things. But he found out that wasn't it. Then he thought maybe life was all about having fun! But he found out that wasn't it either! So then he tried working hard, getting rich, and getting people to like him. But he couldn't find the purpose of life in any of those things either! This was getting frustrating!

Finally, the Teacher discovered where he could find the true purpose of life and he tells us all about it. He didn't find it in any of the ways he tried before. At the end of all his searching, here is what he found. He found that life only has purpose when we have a relationship with God. The Teacher concluded that everything else is a waste of time! And the Teacher should know, he tried everything else!

What do you think life should be all about? Why do you think God put you here?

Think About It

Go through the maze. Try to find your way to the true purpose of life.

TRUTH

Relationship
with God

111

Week 18, Day 3

Finding Jesus in Ecclesiastes

After all his searching, the Teacher in Ecclesiastes finally found the truth. He learned that there is only one true purpose for life. There is only one thing that makes life worth living. He discovered that life only has a purpose when a person has a relationship with God. And that's exactly why Jesus came! Jesus came so that we could have that relationship with God. When we believe in Jesus, he makes us children of God! Then we have a relationship with God that will last forever! Our lives will always be full of meaning, purpose, and blessing!

Jesus said, "I am the way and the truth and the life" (John 14:6). That means Jesus shows us the *way* to have purpose in life. That purpose in life comes from following in the way that Jesus has shown us. Jesus says he is also the *truth*. That means he tells us the truth about our real purpose in life. And Jesus says that he is the *life*. That means that real life is found only in a relationship with Jesus. He gives us eternal life and he explains how we should live as children of God. Jesus saves us from what the Teacher in Ecclesiastes was afraid of.

I AM THE way AND THE truth AND THE life. No one COMES TO THE Father EXCEPT THROUGH me.

—John 14:6

Write About It

Think about the things in your life that make you happy. Write a few of them on the first lines below. Then think about what could cause these things to go away. Write down the things that could do that on each second line.

1. _____   _____

2. _____   _____

3. _____   _____

    A relationship with God gives your life meaning. God sent Jesus so that you could have a relationship with him. When you believe in Jesus, your relationship with God will last forever. Nothing can make it go away! How does that make you feel? Write your thoughts here.

....

....

....

ECCLESIASTES

Pray About It

Dear God,

Thank you for giving my life meaning and purpose! Because I believe in Jesus you have made me your child. My relationship with you will last forever! Nothing can make it go away. What a wonderful thing you have done for me! In the Bible you tell me how to live as your child. Please help me to live that way. I ask for this because I believe in Jesus. Amen.

Ecclesiastes 3:12 says, "I know that there is nothing better for people than to be happy and to do good while they live." Brainstorm some ideas of how you can do good and be happy while you're doing it. Write one idea in each smile below.

Do Something About It

This exploration will remind you of what Ecclesiastes is all about. It will remind you that a relationship with God is the only thing that matters. It's the only thing that will last forever! Everything else will go away.

Get a clear glass cup or a vase. This container represents your life. Now, write down on pieces of white paper the things that fill up your daily life. These might be watching TV, playing with friends, eating, going to school, playing sports, etc. Write one thing on each piece and place them in your glass container.

Now, think of ways you can make God the most important thing filling your life. Write your ideas on the lines below. Then write each idea on a slip of different color paper than you used before. The goal is to replace the white papers in your life container with the colored papers. For example, instead of watching TV every night for a half hour, try reading your Bible or this devotional. You might still play sports. But now you would try to help one of your teammates at every practice. Try to change the color of the papers in your container as each week passes.

....

....

....

....

....

115

Week 19, Day 1

Read About It

God shows us how human love can tell us about his love for us.

Do you love baseball? Maybe. Do you love your parents? Of course! These kinds of love are not the same. And there is a love that is even bigger and greater and more amazing than either of these. That's the love that God has for us!

Song of Songs is a love poem. And there's a reason why God put this love poem in the Bible. He wants us to have a picture of his love for us. He does that by showing us the wonderful love between a husband and a wife! The husband and wife only want what is best for each other. They love each other completely. Their love for each other is amazing! It's the best love human beings can have for each other. And God wants us to know that his love for us is even greater than that!

God is honest and faithful to us. He wants to take care of us. He wants to be with us and do things for us. He only wants what is best for us. He loves us completely! His love for us is amazing! So, the love described in Song of Songs is a picture of God's love for us. And God wants us to love him this way too!

Think About It

Unscramble the underlined words to complete each sentence. These sentences tell what God's love for you is like! If you get stuck, read Song of Songs 8:6–7.

Love is like a <u>gzlibna</u> <u>rfei</u>.

_____ _____

Love burns like a <u>gitmyh</u> <u>melfa</u>.

_____ _____

No amount of <u>rwtae</u> can put it out.

_____

<u>iRrves</u> can't <u>ewesp</u> it away.

_____ _____

Suppose someone offers all their <u>latehw</u> to buy <u>vole</u>.

_____ _____

That won't even <u>moce</u> <u>oselc</u> to being <u>hneugo</u>.

_____ _____ _____

117

Week 19, Day 3

Finding Jesus in Song of Songs

Song of Songs shows us what perfect love between a husband and wife is like. But the love human beings have for each other isn't always perfect. Sometimes we're not honest and faithful to each other. Sometimes we think more about ourselves than other people. Sometimes we don't want what is best for other people. Sometimes we only want to get things rather than give things. But God's love for us is never like that. It's always perfect! It's even better than the perfect love of a husband and wife.

God sent Jesus to show us his amazing and perfect love for us. Jesus showed us how much God loves us by giving his life for us! Would you be willing to die to save someone else's life? If you would, then you must really love that person. That's how much God loves us. Jesus gave everything he had to us. He did that so we could have eternal life. And he did that so we could have a close relationship with God forever. Now there is absolutely nothing standing in the way of God's love for us. And there is nothing keeping us from loving God either. Because of God's love for us, we can give love back to him.

Draw a cross inside this heart. Then color your drawing. Your picture will help you remember how Jesus showed his love for us.

118

Write About It

Song of Songs tells us about God's great love. It tells us that God's love is beautiful and amazing. It tells us that nothing in the whole world can separate us from God's great love! When you believe in Jesus, God's great love is yours! Write how knowing this makes you feel.

....

....

....

Think about some things you could do to show God's love to other people. Write a few of those of those things here.

....

....

....

Week 19, Day 5

Pray About It

Dear God,

Your love for me is amazing! Thank you for loving me so much! I know that you will never stop loving me no matter what happens. I know this because you sent Jesus so that I could have a relationship with you. Now nothing can break my relationship with you. Thank you for loving me so much! Help me to love you more and more. I pray this because I believe in Jesus.

Amen.

Who are you having a hard time loving? Write the name of that person here.

....

Write five ways you can show Jesus' love to this person. This might be hard but it will be worth it!

....

....

....

....

....

Week 19, Day 6

Do Something About It

Love is a beautiful gift from God! God showed us his love by sending his son, Jesus Christ, to earth. Here's something you can do that will help you talk to other people about God's love. For this exploration, you will need an envelope and a pencil or marker. You'll also need a letter opener or scissors.

Carefully open all the flaps of the envelope so it lays open and flat. Use the letter opener or scissors to help you, but don't cut it.

In the center of the opened envelope, write the word LOVE. On the opened flaps, write words that tell what love means. Read 1 Corinthians 13:4–7 for some ideas.

Then fold the flaps to close up the envelope. Write JESUS across the closed flaps. That's because Jesus shows us what God's love looks like.

Use this envelope to remind yourself of God's love. When the envelope is open, you see God's love at the center. And when you believe in Jesus, God's love is at the center of your life. All the actions you wrote describe what God's love is like. These actions should be a part of your everyday life too. Pray to God every day and ask him to help you do these things. God wants to hear from you because he loves you!

121

Week 20, Day 1

Read About It

The holy God challenges his people to honor him.

Would you pet an alligator? Certainly not! Would you invite a grizzly bear to dinner? No way! That's not the right way to act toward them! The right way to act toward them is to stay as far away as possible! What is the right way to act toward God? Have you ever thought about that?

God sent the prophet Isaiah to tell his people how they should act toward God. He said they should honor him with the way they lived their lives. That's how his people can have the best lives possible! But God's people kept doing the opposite. They kept dishonoring God by the way they lived. That wasn't the right way to treat God!

But God is so wonderful that he promised to do something to help his people. God knew his people would always have trouble serving him as they should. So, God would provide someone in the future who would do those things for them. He would be the perfect servant! He would always do what was right! He would always treat God as holy. And God would make that count for us! It would be as though *we* honored God all the time! And this perfect servant would pay the price for our wrong behavior toward God. What wonderful things this perfect servant would do for us!

Think about ways you can treat God as holy and honor him in your daily life. Write them here.

122

Think About It

The verses below tell about things people do that honor or dishonor God. Look up the verses and fill in the blank words. When you're done, read the words from top to bottom to find a message inside the message.

Isaiah 26:13   Your name is the only one we _____.

Isaiah 29:13   _____ _____ says, "These people worship me only with their words."

Isaiah 43:23   You have not honored me _____ _____ sacrifices.

Isaiah 38:16   And my spirit also finds _____ in your promises.

ISAIAH

123

Finding Jesus in Isaiah

God knew that his people would always have trouble honoring him as they should. So, God said he would provide someone in the future who would do those things for them. That person would be the perfect servant.

The perfect servant Isaiah talks about is Jesus! Jesus became a human being to honor God in our place. He became a human being to take God's punishment in our place. When we believe in Jesus, God counts us just as perfect as Jesus is!

God still wants us to honor him. So, God sent the Holy Spirit to help us do what is right. He helps us to honor God. We don't do this because we're afraid of God's punishment. Jesus already experienced God's judgment for us. We honor God because we love him and want to be more like Jesus. Then we'll have the best life possible. And that's what God wants for us!

In which parts of your life can you honor God better? Could you honor God better when you're with your friends? Could you honor God better at school? Write 5 different ideas.

ISAIAH

Write About It

God wants you to honor him, but not because you're afraid of punishment if you don't. Jesus has already experienced that punishment for you! God wants you to honor him because it's something you want to do. Is it something you want to do? Write your thoughts here.

....

....

....

Imagine God came to visit you and followed you around during the day! How would you behave differently? God *does* follow you around during the day! His Holy Spirit is in you! Think of some ways that show you honor God by the way you live. Write them here.

....

....

....

ISAIAH

Pray About It

Dear God,

What an amazing gift you have given to me in Jesus! Thank you so much that he suffered so that I don't have to. You deserve to be honored because you are holy and good. I want to honor you with the way I live. But I still have a hard time with that. Thank you for sending your Holy Spirit to help me to do it. I want to become more like Jesus. Please help me to honor you like Jesus did. I ask this because I believe in him.

Amen.

Isaiah 6:3 says, "Holy, holy, holy is the LORD who rules over all. The whole earth is full of his glory."

Around the words below, create a design that shows this idea.

Do Something About It

Honoring God with our lives sounds like such a big thing. And it is! But big things can get easier when we do them a little bit at a time. So here is a way to make your life honor God one little bit at a time.

Make up your mind today to do one thing to honor God. It doesn't have to be a very big thing. It could be something small. But it should be something you wouldn't usually do. For example, you could clean up after breakfast without being asked. You could say something nice to your brother or sister. You could clean up your room. There are all sorts of things you could do.

Every time you do something to honor God, put a coin in a jar or piggy bank. Every coin will stand for something you did to honor God. See how many coins you can collect during the week. Then on Sunday, put the coins you have collected in the offering at church. It will be your way of saying to God that you honor him. Only you and God will know about it.

127

Week 21, Day 1

Read About It

God must punish our sin but still wants a relationship with us.

God's people weren't listening to him or obeying him. So, God sent the prophet Jeremiah to plead with his people to listen to him. But they acted like they didn't want anything to do with God! This made God very, very sad. He loved his people. He had shown them how to have the best life possible. But they just didn't want to listen to him anymore. So, God had to punish his people. He sent Jeremiah to tell them the bad news. God was going to bring the Babylonians to attack his people. God's people were going to be taken away to a different land. Life was going to be hard for them.

Jeremiah told them that it didn't have to be that way! There was still time for them to come back to God. But they *still* didn't listen to Jeremiah! They didn't think God would punish their sin. So, they left God no choice. He sent the Babylonians against them. The Babylonians won the battle over them and took them to a land far away.

Did a parent or teacher ever tell you not to do something because it was wrong? Did you refuse to listen to them? How did things turn out?

Think About It

JEREMIAH

The prophet Jeremiah talks a lot about our relationship with God. But most of the time he uses a different word than "relationship." This other word means an *official* relationship. It is a relationship that is very, very important to God. See if you can discover that word by unscrambling the letters below.

TOVCNEAN

Did you solve the puzzle? If not, here's a hint for you. The word is found four times in Jeremiah 31:31–33.

Week 21, Day 3

Finding Jesus in Jeremiah

God knew that people would always have a hard time doing what is right. So, God sent the prophet Jeremiah to make a promise to his people. God promised he would provide a perfect human being who would always do what was right. And all the right things that perfect person did would count for everyone who believed in him. That way, God could have that relationship with us that he always wanted. This was really good news!

God sent his own Son, Jesus, to be that perfect person! Jesus always did what was right. And all the right things he did count for everyone who believes in him. Everyone who believes in Jesus can be sure God loves them. In fact, God considers everyone who believes in Jesus to be a member of his family. He calls them his children. That's what the apostle John says in his gospel. Here is what John 1:12 says about Jesus. "Some people did accept him and did believe in his name. He gave them the right to become children of God."

Have you asked Jesus to forgive your sins? Have you asked Jesus to make you a member of his family? If you have, write about when and how that happened.

....

....

....

....

....

Write About It

JEREMIAH

God sent Jesus so he could have a relationship with you that nothing can break. Sin keeps your relationship with God from being everything it can be. But not even sin can break your relationship with God. You are a child of God forever! Write how that makes you feel.

....

....

....

God will always forgive your sin when you ask him to. But sometimes you might not forgive yourself when you sin. Sometimes you might not forgive other people either. They might even have told you they're sorry. Think about some reasons why it might be hard to forgive yourself and other people. Write them here.

....

....

....

Week 21, Day 5

Pray About It

Dear God,

Thank you for loving me so much that you sent your own Son to save me. He gives me a relationship with you that can never be broken! You have forgiven my sins because I trust in Jesus. I am so happy you have made me your child! Help me forgive myself and other people the way you have forgiven me. Help me to love you as much as you love me. Then I'll have the wonderful life that you want for me. I ask you for these things because I believe in Jesus.
Amen.

God forgives you! But that doesn't mean you don't have to do some work when you've done something wrong. Keep the chart below handy for the next time you do something wrong. Follow the steps to make things right again. Remember, it's just as important to forgive others as it is to ask for forgiveness.

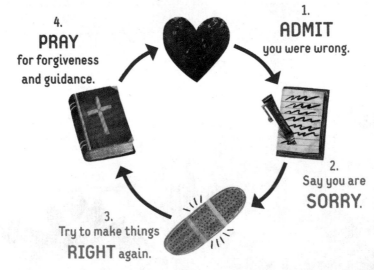

4.
PRAY
for forgiveness
and guidance.

1.
ADMIT
you were wrong.

2.
Say you are
SORRY.

3.
Try to make things
RIGHT again.

Do Something About It

Jeremiah tells us about the special relationship God wants with us. Jesus makes that special relationship with God possible. But we still have to be careful to not let anything come between us and God. Our sins come between us and God. In the space below draw or glue pictures of things that represent your sins. Maybe you could find a photo of people talking together to represent gossip. Or find a picture of money to represent wanting something too much. When you are done, write JESUS across your pictures. This will show you that Jesus keeps those things from separating you from God!

ME   **GOD**

Week 22, Day 1

Read About It

God will never leave us no matter how bad things seem.

God's people didn't listen to him. So, they left God no choice. He sent the Babylonians against them. The Babylonians won the battle over them and took them to a land far away. This was horrible for God's people.

That's why the book of Lamentations was written. Lamentations means "weeping." And there was a lot to weep about! Everything seemed horrible! The temple of God had been robbed and torn down! The palace of the king had been robbed and torn down! The wall of the city had been torn down! All their houses had been torn down! Everything seemed hopeless. Jeremiah told God's people that despite all their sin, God still loved them! Not only that, but God was going to do something amazing for them. God was going to have the relationship with them that he always wanted. And he was going to do something completely new to get it. He was going to send Jesus!

God's people were really having a terrible time. They felt like they were crying all the time. Have you ever felt that way?

Think About It

Read the book of Lamentations. It's one long poem. Then, next to each teardrop write one reason why God's people were sad. Use words from the Book of Lamentations to help you. We've done one for you to get you started.

All those who were chasing them have caught up with them.
—LAMENTATIONS 1:3

Week 22, Day 3

Finding Jesus in Lamentations

Jeremiah wept because God's people were sinning. They were rejecting God. But God is a God of hope. Even when he punishes his people, he brings them hope. Jeremiah reminds readers of God's faithfulness. In Lamentations 3:23–25 he says:

> His great love is new every morning.
> LORD, how faithful you are!
> I say to myself, "The LORD is everything I will ever need.
> So I will put my hope in him."
> The LORD is good to those who put their hope in him.
> He is good to those who look to him.
> It is good when people wait quietly
> for the LORD to save them.

What are God's people waiting for? They are waiting for their deliverer, Jesus.

The verse above says that God's love is new every morning. Tomorrow morning remind yourself how great God's love is. Do this as soon as you wake up. Below, write five things you see and feel that show you God's great love.

....

....

....

....

Write About It

Lamentations is a sad poem. It's OK to be sad. And it does help to admit it. But you don't want to be sad all the time. When you are sad, try to remember all your blessings. Below you will write a poem. It will help you think about being sad but also having many blessings. Use the letters in the word SAD. Write about what makes you sad on the lines by those letters.

S _____

A _____

D _____

Now use the letters in the word BLESSINGS. Write about your blessings on the lines by those letters. That will finish your poem.

B _____

L _____

E _____

S _____

S _____

I _____

N _____

G _____

137

S _____

LAMENTATIONS

Week 22, Day 5

Pray About It

Dear God,

I know that sometimes I do what is wrong. Those things will end up hurting me and making me sad. Thank you for correcting me when I do those things. I know you correct me because you love me. Please help me to stay on the right path. I pray for these things because I believe in Jesus. Amen.

Write a letter to encourage someone you know who is sad. Use some of the words from Lamentations or the poem you wrote to help you. When you are done, rewrite it nicely on paper or in an email and send it off!

....

....

....

....

....

138

Do Something About It

To help encourage others, write the following verse in the frame. Then decorate it. Make copies and hand them out to people who could use cheering up.

> "LORD, I called to you. I called from the bottom
> of the pit. ... You came near when I called out to
> you. You said, "Do not be afraid."
>
> LAMENTATIONS 3:55, 57

139

EZEKIEL

Read About It

God's presence is the key to life.

Have you ever forgotten to water a plant? After a while it starts to wilt. If you don't give it water, soon it will die! God's presence with human beings is like water for plants. We need it to live! That's what God sent the prophet Ezekiel to tell his people. God's people had not paid attention to his presence among them. They had turned away from him. So, they were starting to feel the horrible effects of doing that.

Ezekiel pleaded with the people to return to God. But they continued to turn away from God. So now God was going to turn away from them! Without God's presence, his people would be driven out of their land. They would be taken away as captives to another land. They would no longer have the wonderful life God wanted for them! Like a plant without water, they would begin to die!

Ezekiel also told them of God's grace and mercy. Ezekiel reminded them that new life was still possible if they would turn back to God. It's a life that is full of blessings that lasts forever!

Think about how you would feel if God wasn't present in your life.

Week 23, Day 2
Think About It

With God's presence in your life, you will receive his blessings! Use the "Key" in this exploration to discover some of those blessings. Each verse below has words missing one of the letters in the word "key." Read the verse in the book of Ezekiel to help find the answer. When you do, you will have unlocked a blessing.

1. **Ezekiel 16:62**

   I will mak__ m__ n__w cov__nant with __ou. Th__n __ou will __now that I am th__ LORD.

2. **Ezekiel 34:15**

   I m__s__lf will ta_____ car__ of m__ sh_____p. I will l__t th__m li__ down in saf__t__.

3. **Ezekiel 34:16**

   I will s__arch for th__ lost. I will bring bac__ thos__ who hav__ wand__r__d awa__. I will bandag__ th__ on__s who ar__ hurt. I will ma_____ th__ w__a__ on__s strong__r.

4. **Ezekiel 36:27**

   I will put m__ Spirit in __ou. I will ma_____ __ou want to ob_____ m__ rul__s.

5. **Ezekiel 37:26**

   I will ma_____ a cov__nant with th__m. It promis__s to giv__ th__m p__ac__. Th__ cov__nant will last for__v__r. I will ma_____ th__m m__ p__opl__.

6. **Ezekiel 39:25**

   I will ma_____ sur__ that m__ nam__ is _____pt hol__.

141

Finding Jesus in Ezekiel

True life can only be found in the presence of God. In the book of Ezekiel, God's presence was in the temple. But God caused his presence to come even closer to his people. God became a human being just like us. God's presence was with us in his only Son, Jesus. Here is what the apostle John says about Jesus in John 1:4. "Life was in him." So, the apostle John is telling us the same thing that Ezekiel tells us. Human beings can only find life in God's presence. And Jesus is God's presence. So, true life can only be found in Jesus. Since true life can only be found in Jesus, we need to have a relationship with him. He gives us that relationship when we believe in him. Then we have eternal life!

When you think of your relationship with Jesus, what color comes to mind? You may want to look at Hearty's color chart to help you decide. Then, explain why you chose that color.

....

Draw a picture below to show how you feel about your relationship with Jesus. Be sure to use the color you chose somewhere in your picture.

Write About It

Sometimes you might be like the people Ezekiel spoke to. You might be mean to kids in your neighborhood. You might lie to your friends. You might not want to go to church and worship God. When you do these things, you are turning away from God's presence. Think about how God feels when his people turn away from him. Write your thoughts here.

....

....

....

When you believe in Jesus, you are living in the presence of God. In fact, God's Holy Spirit will live in you! The Spirit will keep you close to God. Write how you feel knowing this.

....

....

....

Pray About It

Dear God,

I love you and want to live in your presence. I know that I find true life there. Please forgive me when I do things that are wrong. Forgive me when I turn away from you. Instead, please help me to have a close relationship with you. I want to show others the wonderful life you give to me. I know I have this life because I believe in Jesus. And because I believe in him, I ask you for these things.
Amen.

What do you think you need to be forgiven for today? Write it inside the heart. Know that God's love will forgive your sins.

Do Something About It

God's presence with you is the key to your life! You can't have true life without it! This exploration will remind you of that.

Go outside and find a large rock. Move the rock to a grassy corner in your yard or garden. Don't move the rock from that spot for a few days. After a few days, move the rock. Look what happened to the grass under it. It will have wilted and may even have started to turn yellow. If you leave the rock there long enough, the grass will die.

The same kind of thing could happen in your relationship with God. If you turn away from God, then you're like the grass under that rock. You are cut off from the life God wants for you. But when you have a close relationship with God, you will have the best life possible! It will be like green grass that grows in the sun.

Take that rock and decorate it. Keep it in your room to remind yourself of this lesson.

145

Week 24, Day 1

Read About It

God shows that he has power and authority over human kingdoms.

Suppose someone was taking you someplace in a car. But while they were driving they took both their hands off the steering wheel! Would you feel safe and secure? Of course not!

Sometimes it might seem like God's not controlling things anymore either! When Daniel lived, it might have seemed like that to some of God's people. That's because the Babylonians had won the battle over them. The Babylonians had taken them away as prisoners to Babylon. Everything God's people had known had changed. They had lost everything they owned. They might have wondered if God was still in control of things!

God used Daniel to bring an important message to his people and the Babylonian king. Daniel brought the same message to the Persian king who came later. God's message to all of them was that he was still in control! And he had always been in control! The kings who ruled over God's people weren't really the ones in charge. That's because God decides who will be king and who won't. Even those kings had to admit that Daniel was right. They admitted that God is more powerful than any king or kingdom! And that's true even if it doesn't seem that way all the time!

Think about times when your life feels out of control. How can you remind yourself that God is still in control?

Think About It

Below are pairs of words. In each pair one word is more powerful than the other. Circle the word that is more powerful. Then, write the first letter of each circled word on the blank lines given below. Write the letters in order from the top to the bottom of the list.

Kings or God
Oak tree or Rose bush
Mouse or Dog
Wood or Iron
Steel or Cardboard
Train or Car
Finger or Hand
Elephant or Ant
Motor bike or Roller skates
Pond or Ocean
Steel or Paper
Motorcycle or Truck
Post or Toothpick
Ox or Kitten
Thread or Wire
Electric drill or Hand drill
String or Rope
Wood or Fire
Universe or Star
Lawn mower or Hand clippers

147

___ ___ ___   ___ ___   ___ ___ ___ ___   ___ ___ ___ ___ ___   ___ ___ ___ ___ ___ ___ ___!

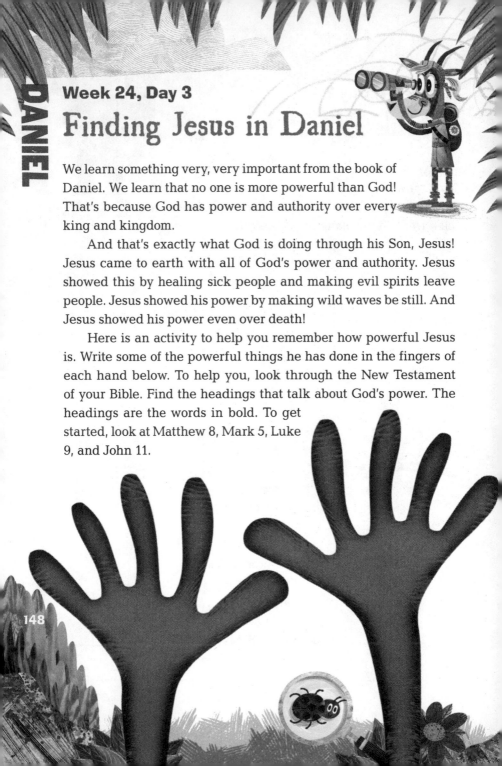

DANIEL

Finding Jesus in Daniel

We learn something very, very important from the book of Daniel. We learn that no one is more powerful than God! That's because God has power and authority over every king and kingdom.

And that's exactly what God is doing through his Son, Jesus! Jesus came to earth with all of God's power and authority. Jesus showed this by healing sick people and making evil spirits leave people. Jesus showed his power by making wild waves be still. And Jesus showed his power even over death!

Here is an activity to help you remember how powerful Jesus is. Write some of the powerful things he has done in the fingers of each hand below. To help you, look through the New Testament of your Bible. Find the headings that talk about God's power. The headings are the words in bold. To get started, look at Matthew 8, Mark 5, Luke 9, and John 11.

148

Write About It

The book of Daniel shows us that God is in control. God has power and authority over everything! God is in control and always will be. Jesus is God's Son. Jesus was given that same power and authority by God. Write how that makes you feel.

....

....

....

There may be times when it will be hard for you to believe God is in control. Daniel trusted that God would give him the strength to do what was right. When you believe in Jesus, he will give you the strength to do what is right too. Write how that makes you feel.

....

....

....

DANIEL

Pray About It

Dear God,

You have all the power and authority in heaven and on earth! You rule over all kings and nations. You are more powerful than anything! That's amazing! But sometimes things don't go well for me. Then I don't always remember you are in control. Please help me to trust in your power and authority. Help me to remember this especially during those hard times. I ask these things because I believe in Jesus. Amen.

Color the words of Daniel 6:10 to remember to pray continually.

He went to HIS ROOM three times a day TO PRAY. He got down on his knees and gave THANKS to his God. -Daniel 6:10

150

Week 24, Day 6

Do Something About It

Go outside for this exploration. It will help you remember that God is more powerful than anything. Find two rocks. Make sure one rock is much bigger than the other. Which rock looks like it's more powerful? The big one of course! The big rock is like the big, bad things that happen to us. The little rock is like us. Suppose we forget God is in control. Then the big, bad things that happen to us can seem more powerful than us!

Pick up both rocks at the same time. Raise them to the level of your chest. Make sure they are at the same height. Let both rocks go at the same time. Which one do you think will hit the ground first? Are you surprised at what happened?

Gravity made both rocks fall at the same speed. That's true even though the bigger rock looked more powerful than the smaller rock! God created gravity, so he is even more powerful! So the next time something looks like it's more powerful than you, remember this. God is more powerful than anything! And God loves you! That's why he sent Jesus!

Week 25, Day 1

Read About It

**God remains faithful to us even
when we are unfaithful to him.**

Has someone ever made a promise to you and then broken it? Maybe it was a friend who broke their promise. Maybe it was even a brother or sister. You thought you could trust that person, but you couldn't. Did it make you angry? Did it make you sad? Now imagine how God feels when his people break their promises to him. That's what the prophet Hosea talks about with God's people.

God sent Hosea to his people to tell them they were being unfaithful. They were not following God's laws and commands. They had broken their promise! They decided they didn't really want a relationship with God! They turned their backs on all the good things God wanted for them. So God would have to punish them. He would bring the Assyrians to win the battle over them. The Assyrians would take all the people away as prisoners. But God still loved his people!

God used Hosea's marriage to show the Israelites their unfaithful behavior. Hosea had married a woman named Gomer. But she was not faithful to Hosea. Even though Gomer was unfaithful and left Hosea, he remained faithful to her. That's because he still loved her. This shows there is hope for God's people too! God will never stop loving them! He is always faithful to us even when we're unfaithful to him!

Have you ever done something wrong? When you did, you turned your back on God. How did that feel? Did you think about how it made God feel?

HOSEA

Think About It

In this exploration, you will discover the words Hosea uses to bring God's message to his people. Fill in the blanks by looking up each verse. Then use the words you find to complete the crossword puzzle.

Across

2. There is no _____ or love in the land. Hosea 4:1
6. Their _____ conduct even makes the king glad. Hosea 7:3
7. _____ us back to you. Hosea 14:2
11. Once again my people will live in the _____ of my shade. Hosea 14:7
14. You have not paid any _____ to my law. Hosea 4:6
15. The time when God will _____ you is coming. Hosea 9:7
16. I will not be so _____ with you anymore. Hosea 11:9
17. You refuse to _____ me. Hosea 5:2
18. They _____ all my laws. Hosea 4:2

Down

1. They have _____ the faithful Holy One. Hosea 11:12
3. I long to _____ them. Hosea 7:13
4. The pride of Israel proves that they are _____. Hosea 7:10
5. I will take good _____ of them. Hosea 14:8

154

8. Now I will _____ them freely. Hosea 14:4
9. Come. Let us _____ to the Lord. Hosea 6:1
10. The ways of the Lord are _____ . Hosea 14:9
11. I am always aware of their _____ . Hosea 7:2
12. They have _____ away from me. Hosea 7:13
13. The people of Israel are _____ . Hosea 4:16

155

Week 25, Day 3

Finding Jesus in Hosea

Hosea continued to love his wife Gomer. He did that even when she was unfaithful to him! In the same way, God continues to love us. He does that even though all of us have been unfaithful to him. Because God still loves us, he sent his son, Jesus. Jesus is completely faithful to God. So Jesus takes away the judgment we deserve.

Hosea and Gomer had three children. Their names sound funny to us but they each mean something important. Their names tell us more about Jesus. The name of Hosea's first child, Jezreel, means "God scatters." God would scatter Israel because of their unfaithfulness. But because of Jesus, God doesn't scatter us! The name of Hosea's second child, Lo-Ruhamah, means "not loved." Because of Israel's unfaithfulness, God would have to treat them like he didn't love them. But because of Jesus' faithfulness, God will always treat us like he loves us! The name of Hosea's third child, Lo-Ammi, means "not my people." Israel's sin had caused God to treat them like they weren't his special people anymore. But Jesus never sinned! So, all those who believe in Jesus will always be called the "people of God."

Have you ever wondered what your name means? Look up the meaning of your name and write it below.

Write About It

Sometimes it seems hard to be faithful to God. We want to do things our way instead of God's way. Think about how you have turned away from God. Maybe you don't always tell the truth. Or maybe you disobey your parents sometimes. How do you feel knowing those things make God sad?

....

....

....

God punished Israel when they were unfaithful to him. But God never stopped loving them! And God brought them back into a right relationship with him. Jesus paid the price for all the times we're unfaithful to God. When we believe in Jesus, he brings us back to God. Because of what Jesus did for us, God never stops loving us. How does knowing this make you feel?

....

....

....

Week 25, Day 5

Pray About It

Dear God,

You have promised you will never stop loving me. But many times, I act like I don't love you. I sin so often that it feels like you can't love me. But you still do! Thank you for loving me so much. Thank you for sending Jesus so that I can always have a close relationship with you. I pray these things because I believe in Jesus.

Amen.

For each letter of the word "faithful" write a way in which you can show your faithfulness to God. Each way must start with the letter shown. Be creative!

F _____

A _____

I _____

T _____

H _____

F _____

U _____

L _____

Do Something About It

This exploration will remind you of Hosea's message.

Go to your room and turn on the light. Now go into the closet. Make sure that, if there is a light in the closet, it is turned off. Put a blanket or towel under the door so that no light can come in. It will be very dark in there! Can you see anything? You might not even be able to see your hand in front of your face! Stay in the closet for a few minutes and then come back out into the light. When you come out, you'll probably have to blink your eyes! The light will seem so bright and so wonderful!

Hosea's wife had done something like this. So had the people of God that Hosea spoke to. Israel had turned away from God. They had chosen to turn away from his instructions. Those instructions were like light in the darkness. But Israel didn't want that light anymore. It was like they had gone into the closet and shut the door on God. But God was still there. His love was still shining toward them. They just had to come out of the darkness to see how bright God's love for them was!

JOEL

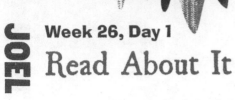

Read About It

The day of the Lord brings judgment and blessing.

Suppose your parents asked you to clean your room. You said you would, but then you forgot. Maybe you wanted to play a video game and lost track of the time. What do you think your parents would say when they saw you hadn't cleaned your room? What if you *had* cleaned your room like they asked? How would they feel then?

The prophet Joel told God's people they hadn't done what God asked. They said they would, but they didn't. They were too busy enjoying all the wonderful things God had given them. So God started taking away those things! He reminded his people that every good thing comes from him. He also reminded them how bad things could become if they were apart from his care. It was a painful lesson to learn. The time when God teaches them to learn this lesson is called "the day of the Lord."

If people have a close relationship with God, the day of the Lord is good news! It's the time when God brings even more blessing to them. But suppose people have turned away from God or have forgotten about him. Suppose they never even had a relationship with God. Then the day of the Lord is bad news! It will be the time when God brings judgment to them. God wants the day of the Lord to be good news for everyone!

160

Do you think the day of the Lord will be good news or bad news for you? Why do you think that?

Week 26, Day 2

Think About It

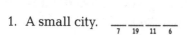

Read each clue and write an answer on the lines.
Notice the number under each letter of the answer.
Write those letters in the matching numbered boxes
in the puzzle. Work back and forth until you solve the puzzle. You
can find the answer in Joel 2:12.

1. A small city. __ __ __ __
   7 19 11 6

2. To give some of what I have to others. __ __ __ __ __
   34 14 24 30 2

3. What ice does on a hot day. __ __ __ __
   41 10 17 27

4. One of four on a car. __ __ __ __
   39 12 25 42

5. The doctor might ask you, "Where does it __ __ __ __?"
   28 4 21 35

6. The opposite of short. __ __ __ __
   3 15 38 16

7. For sweeter iced tea, just add more sugar and then __ __ __ __!
   33 13 40 5

8. 5,280 feet is one __ __ __ __.
   9 32 37 23

9. The opposite of old age. __ __ __ __ __
   18 8 20 26 22

10. One of the Great Lakes. __ __ __ __
    31 1 36 29

1	2	3	4	5	6		7	8		9	10	
11	12	13	14		15	16	17		18	19	20	21
	22	23	24	25	26		27	28	29	30	31	
32	33		34	35	36	37	38		39	40	41	42

161

Finding Jesus in Joel

God wants everyone to have blessings instead of judgment. So he made a way for that to be possible by sending Jesus! Jesus paid the price for all the times we don't do what God told us to do. And when we believe in Jesus, the price he paid counts for us. Jesus does something else for us too. Jesus did everything the Father asked him to do. When we believe in him, all the good things he did count for us too! So now we can have that close relationship with God that he wants for us. And we don't have to worry about judgment on the day of the Lord.

The day of the Lord is the time when Jesus comes back. That's when he will do something about how people have treated God. The day of the Lord will be good news for everyone who trusts Jesus! That's the time when God will give them all the wonderful things he has promised. It will be a time of great celebration!

What do you think the day of the Lord will be like? Write words that describe that day like rays coming out of the clouds.

Write About It

God wants a close relationship with you. God sometimes does things to remind us of that. In the prophet Joel's time, God used a terrible plague of locusts to bring his people back to him. What is God using in your life to remind you of his love for you? Write some things you can think of.

....

....

....

God shows us his love in all kinds of ways. The biggest way he showed us this is by sending Jesus. God never wants us to forget how much he loves us. What are some things you can do to remind yourself that God loves you? Write a few of these things.

....

....

....

Pray About It

Dear God,

You love me so much! But so often I forget to say thank you for everything you have done for me. I forget to spend time with you. I forget to read the Bible or pray to you. You love me so much that you sent your own Son to pay the price for my sin. You want the day of the Lord to be a day of blessing for me and not judgment. You want to have a close relationship with me. Help me to want that too. I ask you for this because I believe in Jesus.
Amen.

This week, keep a record of the time you spend with God. Write down the time you spend praying to him. Write down the time you spend reading and studying God's word. Write down the time you spend in church. There are all sorts of ways to spend time with God!

....

....

....

....

....

Do Something About It

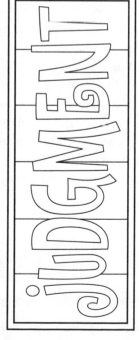

God's people had a hard time understanding what Joel was saying to them. They thought the day of the Lord could only mean blessing for them. They thought they had nothing to worry about. But some of them weren't trusting in God. So, they should have been thinking about judgment instead of blessing! They were mixed up!

Here is something fun you can use to remind yourself of Joel's message. Copy or cut out the two strips below. Glue them together back-to-back to create a bookmark. Put it in the book of Joel in your Bible. Then every time you read Joel you'll remember Joel's message. He is talking about "blessing" for people who are trusting in God and "judgment" for those who are not.

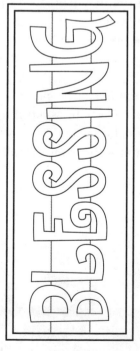

Read About It

God wants us to treat one another like he treats us.

Are you on a team? Maybe you play soccer or volleyball. Even if you're not on a team, you know people who are. People who are on teams usually wear uniforms. That uniform lets everyone know that they're a member of a team.

God sent the prophet Amos to tell his people that they have uniforms too! But their uniform is not the clothes they wear. It's how they live! People should be able to see we're on God's team by what we do. But Amos had to tell God's people they weren't wearing their uniforms! No one could see they were God's people by how they were living! They were being selfish and greedy. They were mean to one another and the people who lived among them. They weren't obeying God and they didn't really mean it when they worshiped him.

God sent the prophet Amos to remind his people how they were supposed to act. They couldn't have God's blessings if they didn't want to be on his team! So, their nation would be destroyed and they would be taken to another country. But even after all that, God would still love them!

How do you show you are on God's team?

Week 27, Day 2

Think About It

When you're on God's team, your life should *reflect* God. This exploration will remind you of that! Each string of letters below doesn't make any sense. But when you look at them in a mirror, then they do! Hold this page in front of a mirror. Read the different ways you can show the truth about God. You'll have to figure out where to divide the sentence into words. Each line will tell you something you can do that God does too!

ALWAYSBEFAITHFUL

DOWHATISRIGHTANDGOOD

BEHONESTWITHEVERYONE

LOVE

BEFAIR

HELPOTHERPEOPLE

BEKINDANDREADYTOFORGIVE

167

AMOS

AMOS

Week 27, Day 3

Finding Jesus in Amos

It seems like the prophet Amos had nothing but bad news for God's people. They weren't living in a way that showed the truth about God. So, God was going to punish them. But even though God was going to punish his people, he would still give them hope. That's because God has so much love and mercy! So, God promised that one day he would bring them back to their land. They would rebuild everything and live in a new community. God's promise to Israel looked forward to another time. That time was when Jesus came to earth to establish a new community of believers!

Jesus showed that new community how they should live and treat one another. And he was the perfect example of this! Jesus' actions and emotions showed us God's great loving care, his mercy, and his justice. When we believe in Jesus, we become members of that new community. We become members of God's team! Our job on this team is to show other people what God is like. We should show people God's love, mercy, and justice in all that we say and do.

Use the space below to draw how you can show other people love, mercy, and justice.

Write About It

Amos tells us about the bad things the Israelites were doing. They didn't respect one another. They were mean and fought with one another. Their lives were not pleasing to God. What would you think if you saw people act like that? Write your thoughts below.

....

....

....

How do you treat your brothers or sisters or kids in your class at school or church? Are you unkind to them? Do you fight with them? Do you ignore them because you think you're better than they are? What do you think Amos would say to *you* about those things? Write your thoughts below.

....

....

....

Week 27, Day 5

Pray About It

Dear God,

I don't always treat my friends fairly. I want things to go my way and be all about me. Sometimes I don't care about other people like I should. Please forgive me for that. Thank you for sending Jesus and for his example to me. He shows me how to be kind and caring. Help me to live so that other people see your love, care, and mercy in me. I ask these things because I believe in Jesus.

Amen.

How can you remind yourself to care for others? Choose a day of the week which will be your day to specifically pray for others. Think of some people you would like to pray for. Write the name of each one of those people on the lines below. Pray for that person on that day of the week. And keep adding weeks and lines and names.

Day 1: _____

Day 2: _____

Day 3: _____

Day 4: _____

Day 5: _____

Do Something About It

God wants us to show what is true about him. Here's a fun way to do that! You'll need two or more people to play. Write these words on 10 small pieces of paper: Love, Mercy, Justice, True, Kind, Fair, Honest, Faithful, Good, Forgive. Each word describes something true about God. Now fold the 10 papers and mix them up. Divide into two teams.

Each team picks five papers. Make sure you don't see what is written on them! Teams take turns playing. When it's their turn to play, a team picks an actor. The actor selects one paper. After they have read the word written on it, start a timer. The actor must use their entire body to spell out the word they just read. It's not fair to use only your hands! Form one letter at a time. Everyone else on their team has to guess the word the actor is spelling. When they get it right, stop the timer. Record how long it took the team to guess the word. Keep switching back and forth until both teams have finished their five words. Add up the total time it took each team to guess their words. The team with the shortest amount of time wins!

In this game, you showed people truths about God. He wants you to do that every day!

HELLO! NICE TO MEET YOU!

Week 28, Day 1

Read About It

God is the only one who is able to judge fairly.

Have you ever wanted to get back at somebody? Maybe you thought they needed to be taught a lesson. And maybe you thought you were the one to do it! That's what the Edomites thought about God's people. God sent the prophet Obadiah to talk about that.

The Babylonians were attacking God's people, and the Edomites were happy about it! They thought God's people deserved it. That's because the Edomites had been ruled by God's people for many years. And they didn't like it one bit! Now the Edomites were happy God's people were having such a hard time. But the Edomites didn't see the whole picture.

They only saw part of the picture. But they were ready to give God's people a failing grade. The Edomites thought it was fair and right to be mean to the Israelites. They forgot that only God can see the whole picture. He is the only one who can judge fairly.

Have you ever been happy because someone else was sad? Be honest. Why do you think you felt that way? How can you stop yourself from feeling that way again?

Think About It

Here's a way for you see what the prophet Obadiah is talking about. Sometimes we think we understand something but later we learn that our understanding was wrong. Look at the picture on the left. It has a red circle in the center that is inside bigger circles. Now look at the picture on the right. It has a red circle in the center of smaller circles. Which red circle is bigger?

It might surprise you to learn that both red circles are the same size. The smaller circles around the red circle on the right have tricked your eyes. Only God sees things as they really are. So only he is able to make the right judgments all the time.

Finding Jesus in Obadiah

The Edomites were judging God's people unfairly. They didn't know everything that God was doing. And the Edomites didn't have the right to judge anybody anyway! That right belongs to God alone.

People also judged Jesus unfairly. They didn't understand who Jesus was. They didn't see the whole picture. So, they judged him according to their own understanding. But their own understanding was wrong! Jesus didn't make this same mistake. He didn't try to get back at the people who were being mean to him. Instead, he trusted that God would judge them fairly. In 1 Peter 2:23 the apostle Peter describes what Jesus did. Here is how he describes it. "People shouted at him and made fun of him. But he didn't do the same thing back to them. When he suffered, he didn't say he would make them suffer. Instead, he trusted in the God who judges fairly."

Think about someone you might be judging unfairly. You don't have to write down their name. But think of some reasons why you might be judging them unfairly. Write those in the small box on the left. In the box on the right, write ways that you can think of them more fairly. Make sure you fill up that box. Make sure you write more positive things than negative.

174

Write About It

Think about a time someone said something about you that wasn't true. Maybe they thought you were being mean but you weren't. Maybe they thought you said something negative about them, but you hadn't. How did that make you feel? Write your thoughts here.

....

....

....

Now what about you? Maybe you've done the same thing to someone. Maybe you believed something about someone that you later learned wasn't true. How did that make you feel? Write your thoughts below.

....

....

....

OBADIAH

Pray About It

Dear God,

You are the only one who is able to judge fairly. Please forgive me for judging other people even though I don't know everything. I am glad you don't judge me the way I judge other people! You are loving and forgiving. You're always fair and do what is right. Please help me to be more like you. Help me to leave all the judging to you. Only you know everything and everyone perfectly! I ask for these things because I believe in Jesus.

Amen.

In the space below create an emoji that shows how you think others might feel when you judge them unfairly.

Now, create an emoji that shows how you would like to make others feel.

Do Something About It

Human beings are often prideful. This means we find fault with other people but think what we are doing is great. It's much easier to find fault with others than look at ourselves and make changes. Here is something you can do the next time you find fault with someone. Use the chart below to remind yourself that they are a lot like you. Challenge yourself to think of 10 ways you are similar. There are two to get started.

Is this person like me?	YES →	How is this person like me?

NO ↓

Think again. Go back and start over.

↓

1. They go to my school.

2. They live in the same city.

3. _____

4. _____

5. _____

6. _____

7. _____

8. _____

9. _____

10. _____

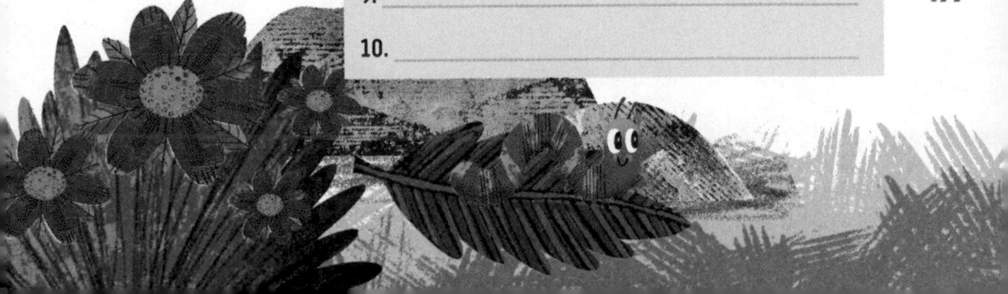

Week 29, Day 1

Read About It

God's love and care for people have no limits.

Has anyone ever done something really mean to you or your family or friends? You might have wished that something bad would happen to those mean people! If you've ever thought that, then you can understand how the prophet Jonah felt.

The Assyrians had been very, very mean to the Israelites. But God told Jonah to go to their capital city of Nineveh to preach to them. God wanted them to stop sinning so he could bless them. But Jonah wanted God to punish the Assyrians, not bless them! So, Jonah tried to sail away on a ship. But God created a storm that kept the ship from getting away. Then God created a great fish to swallow Jonah. After three days the fish brought Jonah back to dry land and spat him out. Jonah got up, cleaned himself off, and did what God said. Jonah went to the Assyrians and told them to stop sinning. Then something else amazing happened! The Assyrians listened to Jonah and did what he said!

Jonah wasn't happy about this at all! So God decided that Jonah needed to learn something more. Jonah needed to learn that all of us deserve to be punished for doing bad things. But God wants to bless us instead. And if God blesses us, why shouldn't he bless other people too? God's love and care for people have no limits.

God wants to bless everyone. He even wants to bless people we might not like. How does that make you feel?

Think About It

Jonah tried to put a limit on God's love. So Jonah ran away on a ship. But the sailors threw him into the Mediterranean Sea. How many words can you find in the word MEDITERRANEAN? List all the words with three letters or more that you can find. There are over 100! See what your limit is!

MEDITERRANEAN

179

Week 29, Day 3

Finding Jesus in Jonah

God showed Jonah that everybody deserves God's judgment and blessing. If God only blessed the people who deserved it, then nobody would be blessed! But God is so wonderful and good! He made a way to punish everyone's sin and bless them at the same time! That shows how much God loves us and wants a close relationship with us.

God showed us just how much he loves all of us by sending his Son, Jesus. Like Jonah, Jesus came to tell us to turn away from sin and turn to God. But unlike Jonah, Jesus didn't run away from his task. He showed us God's love in spite of the mean things we've done. Not only that, but Jesus experienced the punishment that all of us deserve. He did that so when we trust in Jesus God can bless us. Isn't that amazing! There is no limit to God's love!

Think of some ways you can tell others about Jesus. Write your ideas in the thought bubbles.

Write About It

Think about all the bad things you've done in your life. It might be hard for you to believe that God loves you. But he does! In fact, he loves you so much that he sent his Son to die for you. Write here how this makes you feel.

....

....

....

Maybe you have a hard time with some people. Maybe they've done mean things to you. So you don't want to be nice to them. But you've done those same things to God and he still loves you! How could you show God's love to people you have a hard time with? Write your ideas here.

....

....

....

JONAH

Pray About It

Dear God,

Sometimes I've been just like the prophet Jonah. I'm happy you love me. But I'm not so happy you love some other people. I know that's not right. You don't have any limits on your love. All we have to do is believe in Jesus. He's the only one who is perfect. So, he can represent all the rest of us who are not perfect. Please help me to be more like you. Help me to not put limits on my love either. I ask you for this because I believe in Jesus.

Amen.

Sometimes we might not want God to bless other people. But we know from reading Jonah that God wants to bless everyone who asks him for forgiveness. Think of people you might not want God to bless. Write their names in the heart below. Focus your prayer on those people this week. Pray that they will ask God to forgive their sin. Then God can bless them as he has blessed you!

Week 29, Day 6

Do Something About It

The prophet Jonah tried to put a limit on God's love. Jonah wanted God to love only the people Jonah thought deserved it. But nobody deserves God's love! God loves people who don't deserve it. And that includes Jonah! Jonah needed to learn God's love for people has no limits.

This exploration will remind you of what Jonah needed to learn. Take an empty plastic water bottle and fill it with water. Fill it all the way to the top. Then twist on the lid. Make sure the lid is on tight. Now put the full water bottle in the freezer. Let it stay there all night.

In the morning, check out what happened to the water bottle.

When the water froze, it got bigger. But there was no room for it to get bigger inside the bottle. Perhaps the bottle burst or expanded and pushed out the sides or bottom. God's love is just like that water! You might sometimes think some people don't deserve God's love. If you do, remember what happened to the bottle you put into the freezer. Some things can't be held back. They have no limits. God's love is like that!

Week 30, Day 1

Read About It

God must punish his people when they disobey, but he will still bless them.

Have you ever had a cavity in your tooth? It can hurt a lot. When you get a cavity, you have to go to the dentist. To fix your tooth, you'll have to experience some pain. If you don't do something about it, the problem could get a whole lot worse!

That's like what God sent the prophet Micah to tell his people. Micah had to tell them their behavior was rotten. And just like a cavity, something had to be done about it. But their behavior was worse than a cavity. Micah describes it as a plague! You can read what he says in Micah 1:9. God could have just let his people suffer because of their sin. But God loved them too much for that.

Micah had a scary message for God's people. He told them that God was going to let another nation have the victory over them. Then they would be taken as prisoners to another land. It was going to be very painful. But it was the only way to get their attention. It was the only way to get them to turn back to God. But God talks about a wonderful blessing that will come after he punishes their sin. He will show mercy and bless them once more. How great is that!

Think about a time you may have been punished. It was probably hard at the time. But what did you learn from it?

Think About It

MICAH

The Israelites had turned away from God. So, God had to punish them. But then God did something nobody expected. He promised to bless his people again in the future! This puzzle helps you to follow the Israelites from judgment to blessing.

For this challenge, you'll start out with a negative word. Then you must change one letter at a time. Each time you change a letter, you have to end up with a real word. The goal is to end up with a positive word. We've helped you with the first one.

1. SAD → BAD → BAN → FAN → FUN

2. CRY → __ __ __ → __ __ __ → __ __ __ → JOY

3. HIT → __ __ __ → __ __ __ → PAL

4. LIE → __ __ __ → __ __ __ → __ __ __ → __ __ __ → AWE

5. MAD → __ __ __ → __ __ __ → GOD

Finding Jesus in Micah

The prophet Micah had to bring some painful news to God's people in the Old Testament. He told them that God was going to punish them for their sin. It was going to be painful, but it had to be done. God wanted them to have the best life possible. But that couldn't happen when sin kept getting in the way. So, God was going to do something about it.

The God in the New Testament is the same God as in the Old Testament! He still punishes sin. But God has provided a way for all this punishment to be taken care of. God sent Jesus to experience all the punishment for us! Jesus suffered and died to pay for all our sin. Now we don't have to be punished for our sin if we believe in Jesus! Just imagine that! God was angry with the sin of the Israelites. So just imagine how angry he is at the sin of every person who ever lived! That's what Jesus experienced for everyone who trusts in him!

Read Micah 2:1–5. How does this passage make you feel?

Write your feelings on the cross. Then remember that Jesus died to pay for all your sins! Now you don't need to worry about God's judgment.

186

MICAH

Write About It

MICAH

The prophet Micah told God's people they had turned away from God. They worshiped God without really meaning it. They stole things. They cheated people. They treated one another badly. Maybe you've done things that you aren't proud of. Write to God about them here.

....

....

....

God loves you so much that he sent Jesus. Jesus paid the price for your sin. All you have to do is believe in him. Then you will never have to worry about God's judgment. How does God's great love for you make you feel? Write your thoughts below.

....

....

....

MICAH

Week 30, Day 5

Pray About It

Dear God,

I know that I've done many of the same things the Israelites did. I am so sorry about those things. Your love is amazing! You sent Jesus to pay the price for my sins so that I wouldn't have to. Please help me not to forget your great love for me. Please guide me by your Holy Spirit so that I become more like Jesus. Help me to live in a way that shows you how thankful I am. I know I can ask you for these things because I am trusting in Jesus.

Amen.

Fill in the chart below to help you focus your prayers this week.

I am sorry for ...	Forgive me for ...	Guide me ...

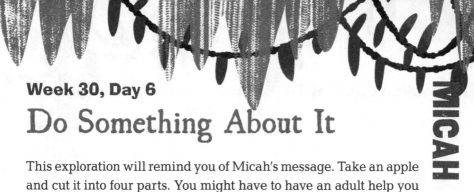

Week 30, Day 6

Do Something About It

This exploration will remind you of Micah's message. Take an apple and cut it into four parts. You might have to have an adult help you with this. After you cut the apple, leave the pieces on the counter for an hour. Don't cover them. Just leave them out in the open.

After an hour, see what has happened to the apple. Draw a picture of it here.

The apple has probably started to turn brown. If something isn't done about the apple, the whole thing will rot! And if something wasn't done about the Israelites, their sin would have destroyed them! God had to cut the sin out of the Israelites.

That apple is going to need some cutting done to it as well. The pieces don't look great right now. But if you cut the brown off, they'll look much better.

This is a way to think about what Jesus did. He experienced God's judgment. He experienced all the cutting for us. Now we look like people who make God happy. The judgment of Jesus results in our blessing. That's a pretty deep thing for you to think about!

189

NAHUM

Read About It

God rules over all and will judge his enemies.

Have you ever studied something in school and then forgotten what you learned? When you were first learning it, it probably all made sense to you. You thought you knew it well. But later you had to write about it or take a test on it. And you realized you didn't really know it after all!

The Assyrians thought they knew about the God of Israel and Judah. Years before, God had sent the prophet Jonah to them. Jonah had warned them to stop sinning! And they did! It seemed like they had learned their lesson. But it didn't take long before it became clear they hadn't really learn it at all. They started sinning again. Now the Assyrians had turned completely away from God. They had even fought against God's people! Now God would fight against them! The Assyrians had become the enemy of God's people. That meant they were God's enemy too!

Nahum's message to the Assyrians was not about God's mercy and forgiveness. His message was that God rules over all and will judge his enemies. Nahum told the Assyrians that God was finished with them. God would punish them for their sins! They would experience God's great anger and judgment! It would be terrible! God would destroy them! No one would escape! The Assyrians would learn that God alone rules over all! And this is a lesson they would never forget!

190

How do you think you would feel if you learned God was finished with you?

Think About It

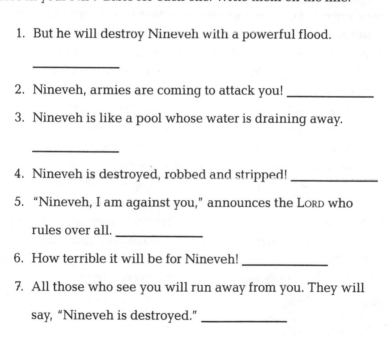

NAHUM

Nineveh was the capital of Assyria. Nahum makes many prophesies about Nineveh. Some of Nahum's prophecies are listed below. Find the chapter and verse in your NIrV Bible for each one. Write them on the line.

1. But he will destroy Nineveh with a powerful flood.

   _____

2. Nineveh, armies are coming to attack you! _____

3. Nineveh is like a pool whose water is draining away.

   _____

4. Nineveh is destroyed, robbed and stripped! _____

5. "Nineveh, I am against you," announces the LORD who

   rules over all. _____

6. How terrible it will be for Nineveh! _____

7. All those who see you will run away from you. They will

   say, "Nineveh is destroyed." _____

Week 31, Day 3

Finding Jesus in Nahum

God rules over all and will judge evil people. That's the lesson the prophet Jonah had taught the Assyrians. But they had forgotten all about it! Now because of their evil ways, the Assyrians would experience God's judgment. They could not escape it. There was no safe place for them. That's a scary thing to think about! That's because all of us have forgotten about God at some point in our lives! All of us have done evil things too.

But God has provided a place of protection against his judgment. That place of protection is Jesus. Jesus experienced God's anger and judgment against our sin in our place. So when we believe in Jesus, we have complete protection from God's judgment.

But what about the people who don't believe in Jesus? They are outside of the place of protection that Jesus gives. What a scary place to be! When Jesus comes again, those people will experience God's judgment against them. But everyone who believes in Jesus doesn't have to worry. Jesus doesn't bring them punishment. Jesus brings them life filled with peace, safety, and joy.

Under the hat write all of the things that Jesus protects you from.

Write About It

One day all people will be judged by God for the way they live. This is hard to talk about, but it's true! Think about your life. How do you feel knowing that God looks at the way you live?

....

....

....

When you believe in Jesus, he pays for the wrong things you do. The judgment he already experienced counts for you. You are forgiven and made perfect in God's eyes! Jesus will come again to judge the world. So, when he comes again, you won't have to experience God's judgment. You will be protected and safe. Write how that makes you feel.

....

....

....

Week 31, Day 5

Pray About It

Dear God,

You rule over all! And you are the judge of all! That's an awesome thought! It's scary knowing that I do wrong things. Thank you for sending Jesus. Because I believe in Jesus, I know that the wrong things I do are forgiven. And I know I will not be judged for them! I want my life to show how much I love you! I also pray for all those people who do not know Jesus. Please help them believe in Jesus too. I pray these things because I believe in Jesus!

Amen.

On the signs below, write some ways that you can point others toward knowing Jesus.

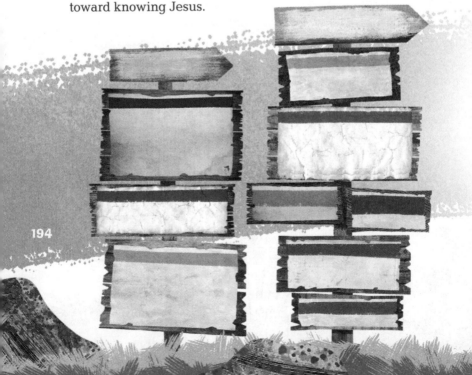

Do Something About It

This exploration will help you see what the prophet Nahum is talking about!

Sprinkle some pepper in the bottom of a white bowl or mug. Then cover the pepper with sugar cubes. The sugar cubes are like the Assyrians. The pepper is like God's people in the time of the prophet Nahum. They were suffering under the weight of the evil Assyrians. Now pour hot water over the sugar cubes. That's like God pouring out his judgment against the evil Assyrians. They were the enemies of God and the enemies of his people. See how the sugar cubes melt when the hot water is poured on them. In the same way God's enemies will melt when his judgment is poured out on them.

But God's people have nothing to worry about! God's judgment won't affect them. Notice how the pepper doesn't melt when you pour the hot water on it. In fact, the pepper comes to the surface! The hot water doesn't hurt it at all. That's exactly what the prophet Nahum is saying. Here is what he says about God in Nahum 1:7–8. "He takes good care of those who trust in him. But he will destroy Nineveh with a powerful flood." God will always take good care of those who trust in him!

195

Week 32, Day 1

Read About It

God is our only comfort and joy in hard times.

Maybe you've seen other kids cheat or fight. Or maybe you've seen a big kid bully someone. Maybe you've even seen someone take something from the store and not pay for it! Don't things like that make you upset? Don't you wish someone would do something about it?

The prophet Habakkuk was also upset. The people of Judah weren't living like God's people should live. They weren't treating one another fairly. They argued and fought all the time. They were living evil lives. It seemed to Habakkuk that there was no one to stop the evil people. He couldn't understand why this was happening. Why didn't God do something about it?

So Habakkuk asked God to do something. But God answered him in a way he didn't expect! God said he would punish the people of Judah. He would do that by letting the evil Babylonians win the battle over them. But that answer didn't make Habakkuk feel any better! Why would God use the evil Babylonians to punish his own people? But God told Habakkuk that he didn't need to worry about that. God said he would also punish the Babylonians in the future. Their kingdom wouldn't last. So Habakkuk was reminded that his comfort and joy should be in God alone.

How do you remind yourself that God is in control and all that you need?

Think About It

Habakkuk had a lot of bad things to deal with. See how many bad things are listed in Habakkuk 3:17!

> The fig trees might not bud.
> The vines might not produce any grapes.
> The olive crop might fail.
> The fields might not produce any food.
> There might not be any sheep in the pens.
> There might not be any cattle in the barns.

All these things might be true, but Habakkuk could still have joy! How could that be possible? How could Habakkuk have joy when everything in his life seemed to be going wrong? Solve the puzzle below to see how. Count the letters in the verse above. Write the letter that matches each number in the puzzle blanks below. Count carefully. The first letter is done for you.

G _ _ _ _ _ _ _ _ _ _ _ _ _ _ _ _ _ _
6 18 22   27 30   37 43 50   58 90 59 48   157 118 144 103 150 170 76

197

Finding Jesus in Habakkuk

Habakkuk was upset because so many things were going wrong. God's people weren't following God. Evil people seemed to be having success. Nothing seemed to be right! All these things made him very sad. Habakkuk wondered if God was still in control. Habakkuk had to be reminded that God was the one who would never disappoint him. Everything around Habakkuk might change for the worse, but God never would. He would always love Habakkuk! And God's good plans for his people will succeed no matter what!

When Jesus came, God's people were struggling like Habakkuk. Everything seemed to be going wrong. God's people needed to be reminded again that God was still in control. They needed to know that God's power had not changed and does not change! Jesus showed that God was still powerful by performing many miracles. And Jesus reminded everyone that true rest came from having a close relationship with him. Here is how Jesus said that in Matthew 11:28–29. "Come to me, all you who are tired and are carrying heavy loads. I will give you rest. Become my servants and learn from me. I am gentle and free of pride. You will find rest for your souls."

Is there something that seems to be going wrong in your life right now? Draw or write about it on the cross. Then let Jesus take care of it.

Week 32, Day 4

Write About It

HABAKKUK

Sometimes we are like Habakkuk. We feel that life is unfair and hard. That makes us sad! That's when we need to remember that God is in control and he cares for us. Write how knowing this makes you feel.

....

....

....

Habakkuk worried about things and had lots of questions. So he talked with God about his questions. When you believe in Jesus, you have a close relationship with God. So you can ask God all your questions too! Write five questions you'd like to ask God.

....

....

....

....

....

Week 32, Day 5

Pray About It

Dear God,

I know that you are in control. My comfort and joy are found in you. But sometimes life is hard. Sometimes I even see your own people doing bad things. That makes me sad! But I know I can talk with you about what makes me sad. Help me to focus on you and your promises to me. Then I can be patient and trust you completely. I know that when I do that I'll have real comfort and joy! I ask these things because I believe in Jesus.

Amen.

Color Matthew 11:28 to help you remember.

Come to me, ✳✳✳ all you who are TIRED ✳✳✳ and are carrying HEAVY LOADS. ✳✳✳ i will give you REST.

—MATTHEW 11:28

200

Do Something About It

Habakkuk worried about a lot of things that were happening around him. Things weren't going as he would have liked. Habakkuk needed to be reminded that God was still in control. God knows what he is doing. We can trust him even when we're having hard times.

Imagine that you could write a letter to Habakkuk to cheer him up. You could remind him that his true joy in life comes from his relationship with God. And God will always be there for him, no matter what is happening around him! Write Habakkuk a short letter to encourage him. When you're done, put it in an envelope.

Maybe you know someone else who is having a hard time. They might need to be reminded that God is still in control and loves them too. You could give this letter to them. It would help them remember where they can find comfort and joy even in hard times. Or maybe *you* need to read your own letter the next time you begin to worry!

201

Week 33, Day 1

Read About It

God wants us to be ready when he comes to judge the world.

Are you ready? You may hear these words often. Sometimes you may not pay any attention to them!

The prophet Zephaniah asked God's people if they were ready. They needed to be ready because God was coming to judge them. But God's people didn't pay attention to Zephaniah's warning. That's because their enemies weren't bothering them. God's people thought they were safe. They thought they didn't need to follow God's ways. So, they turned away from the true God and worshiped false gods. They followed the evil ways of other nations. They thought God would never be angry with them or punish them because of those things.

So, Zephaniah's message blew them away! He said the day of God's judgment was going to come for God's people! They would be destroyed. Only those people who trusted in God would be safe from the fury of his judgment! How scary is that!

Do you ever feel scared about God's judgment? Why or why not?

Think About It

ZEPHANIAH

We know God is coming again. And we need to be ready. When you complete this figure, you will have a reminder of what you need to be ready.

Read the question and circle the letter by the item that answers the question the best. On the figure below connect the letter of the question to the letter of the best answer. Then, draw a line that connects the two letters. Do the same thing for all the questions. After you have all the lines drawn, look at the figure you created. Do you recognize it? It will remind you to believe in Jesus and be safe in his protection. Then you will be ready when he comes to judge the world!

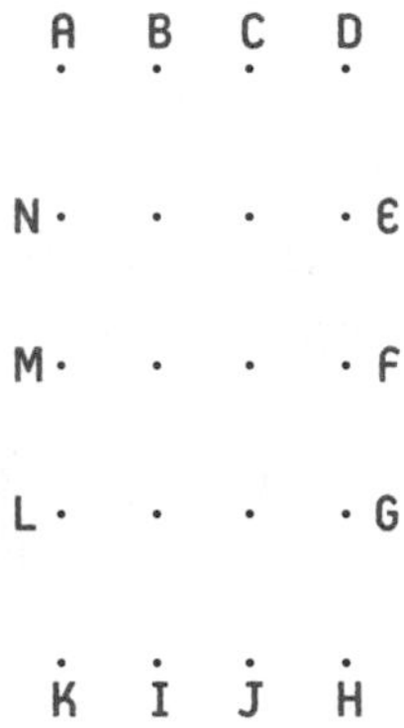

B. What do you need to be ready to go to school?
   A. blanket   D. bucket   I. backpack

C. What do you need to be ready for the beach?
   J. swimsuit   M. bike   G. snow shovel

N. What do you need to be ready to ride your bike?
   K. snow boots   E. helmet   H. sandwich

M. What do you need to do to be ready for supper?
   F. kite   D. play a video game   F. wash your hands

C. What do you need to be ready to play baseball?
   K. candy   B. bat   L. rake

N. What do you need to be ready to read?
   E. bike   M. book   G. camera

F. What do you need to be ready to go to church?
   A. your desk   J. your dog   E. your Bible

I. What do you need to be ready for Jesus' coming?
   E. money   J. believe in Jesus   G. nothing

A B C D

N   E

M   F

L   G

K I J H

Week 33, Day 3

Finding Jesus in Zephaniah

Zephaniah told God's people in Judah that the day of God's judgment was coming. God would judge the whole world including them. Their only chance was to return to God and find protection in him. If they didn't, they would experience God's judgment.

A New Testament prophet, John the Baptist, brought a similar message. His message was for a different group of listeners, and that includes us. John also talked about God's coming judgment and the way to escape it. Jesus is coming again with God's judgment. But Jesus is also the way to escape God's judgment!

When someone believes in Jesus, the punishment he experienced counts for them! So instead of God's punishment, they find the best life possible. They also find safety from God's judgment when Jesus comes again. But if someone doesn't believe in Jesus, they will have to pay for their own sins. Why would anyone choose to do that? Believe in Jesus and enjoy his gift of wonderful life!

In the space below, write how you would tell someone why they should believe in Jesus.

Week 33, Day 4

Write About It

God will come to judge the world and all the people in it. We don't know when he is coming but we know he will. That sounds very scary! How does knowing God will come again make you feel? Are you ready? Write your thoughts below.

....

....

....

Jesus has given us the way to escape God's judgment. That's because Jesus has already paid the price for all our sin. If you believe in Jesus, you will be ready on the day God judges the world. Write how that makes you feel.

....

....

....

Pray About It

ZEPHANIAH

Dear God,

You are mighty and powerful. You rule over all the earth. I know you will come again to judge it. Sometimes that makes me afraid. But I don't need to be afraid because I believe in Jesus. I believe he has paid for all my sin. I believe that Jesus will protect me and keep me safe on judgment day. Thank you for sending Jesus to keep me safe. I pray these things because I believe in Jesus.
Amen.

For each letter in the word "afraid" below, write a way that Jesus helps you not to be afraid. Each reason must start with that letter.

A _____

F _____

R _____

A _____

I _____

D _____

Do Something About It

Create this game to play with four other people. Get 4 blank 3 x 5 index cards. Draw a cross on one of the cards. Write "Horrible Trouble" on the other cards.

Turn the index cards over so no one can see what is written on them. Mix them up. Have everyone stand in a circle. Deal one card to each person but they can't look at the card. Here is the sentence you'll say. "The Lord is coming to judge us all."

Start with the first person on your left. Point to that person and say, "The." Point to the second person on your left and say, "Lord." Keep going around the circle until you've said the whole sentence. The last person you point to has to turn over their card. If their card has the cross drawn on it, they're safe! But if their card has "Horrible Trouble" written on it, they're out! Take that person's card and set it aside. Now collect the cards from everyone who remains and mix them up again. Make sure no one sees what is written on the cards. Give everyone a card again and repeat what you did before.

Keep playing the game until only one person is left. That person's card will have the cross drawn on it. The cross reminds everyone of the prophet Zephaniah's message. The Lord is coming to judge us all! Only people who trust in Jesus will be safe.

Week 34, Day 1

Read About It

**God wants his people to put
him first in their lives.**

In the time of the prophet Haggai, the people of God had started rebuilding God's temple. But they hadn't finished it. It was hard work! They wanted to build their own houses instead. And the people who lived around them didn't want them to build the temple anyway. God's people had all sorts of excuses for not building God's temple. But not one of those excuses was very good.

Haggai told God's people that rebuilding the temple would show something true about them. It would show that they loved God and put him first in their lives. If they obey God, he will bless them.

Have you ever started your homework but didn't finish it? Why did that happen? Did you get tired of it? Did it become too hard for you? Did something else seem more important?

Think About It

HAGGAI

God's people listened to what the prophet Haggai said. Haggai 1:14 tells us what they did. "Then everyone began to work on the temple of the LORD who rules over all. He is their God." When they did this, they were doing something else too. This exploration will help you to see what that was!

Start at the left tent. Write the numbers that are in that tent under the blank spaces for the first word below. Make sure to write them in order. Then move to the next tent and do the same thing. Do this for all three tents. The numbers stand for the letters in verse 1:14 above. Just count the letters in the verse until you come to the number under the blank. Then write that letter in the blank space above the number. When you're done, you'll have Haggai's message for God's people!

32   48   1   15   10   70   36   61   8   51   18

209

Week 34, Day 3

Finding Jesus in Haggai

God's people in Haggai's time had forgotten what was most important. They were supposed to be rebuilding God's temple. That's the way they could show they were putting God first in their lives.

Jesus always put the work of God the Father first in his life. Here is what Jesus says in John 4:34. "My food is to do what my Father sent me to do. My food is to finish his work."

How are you putting God first in your life? How could you do that better? Write your thoughts below.

....

....

....

....

....

210

Write About It

God's people during Haggai's time had let many things take their attention away from God. What things might be taking *your* attention away from God? Write some of them below.

....

....

....

You can tell people about God using words or by how you live. When you do, you will be helping to build God's new temple, the church. Think about ways you can tell or show people the truth about God. Write your thoughts below.

....

....

....

HAGGAI

Pray About It

Dear God,

Please forgive me for sometimes letting other things make me forget about you. Please help me to live in a way that shows you are most important to me. Help me to join with Jesus in building your new temple, the church. I ask you for these things because I believe in Jesus.
Amen.

Believers help to build God's new temple by telling other people about Jesus. Think about some ways you could do that. Write your ideas below.

....

....

....

Do Something About It

HAGGAI

Haggai wanted God's people to put God first. Think of five activities that might keep you from putting God first. Write them in the clouds below. These might include things like video games, sports, or hanging out with friends. Clouds can block out the sun. And these things can block out God in your life. Under each cloud write how you will put God first in that activity. Then the clouds won't block out God anymore and you'll be putting God first!

213

Read About It

God wants the place he lives to show what is true about him and his people.

Just like Haggai, the prophet Zechariah encouraged God's people to rebuild the temple. But he did it by telling them about something else rebuilding the temple would show. It would show something true about God. It was a way to show God's desire to be present with his people. And God's desire to be present with his people points to the future. At that time God would be even more present with his people by sending his Son!

Rebuilding the temple had so much to show about God's people and about God. That's why it needed to be rebuilt!

If you had to build a temple for God, what would it look like?

Think About It

ZECHARIAH

Zechariah told God's people why it was important to rebuild the temple. The temple would show everyone true things about God's people. It would also show true things about their God who was with them.

Seven ways to describe God are provided below. Next to each one is a blank. Here is something you can do during the seven days of this week. On each day of the week think about one of the words that describes God. Then write down one thing you did that showed other people that true thing about God. When you do these things during the week, you'll be showing people who God is. And God will use what you do to build his new temple, the church!

GIVING _____

LOVING _____

GOOD _____

KIND _____

PATIENT_____

PURE _____

FAITHFUL_____

Week 35, Day 3

Finding Jesus in Zechariah

Just like the people in Zechariah's day, Jesus is building God's temple! But the temple Jesus is building is different. It is made up of all the people who believe in Jesus! In other words, it's the church! God was present with his people in the temple in Old Testament times. Now God is always present with his people in the church because of Jesus. His Holy Spirit lives in everyone who believes in Jesus!

The apostle Paul even calls the church God's temple! Here is what he asks believers in 1 Corinthians 3:16. "Don't you know that you yourselves are God's temple?" Did you ever think of yourself as a temple?

How can you help build God's temple by the way you live? Write an idea in each building block.

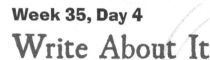

Write About It

ZECHARIAH

Create a book to help you remember the main ideas in Zechariah. In the boxes below, draw pictures to show each important idea. Cut the boxes apart and staple them together to create a book.

GOD LIVES AMONG HIS PEOPLE.

GOD'S PEOPLE SHOULD BE BUILDING HIS TEMPLE.

THE TEMPLE SHOWS WHAT GOD IS LIKE.

GOD'S PEOPLE SHOW WHAT GOD IS LIKE.

Week 35, Day 5

Pray About It

Dear God,

Thank you for choosing to be present with your people always. Please help me to live in a way that shows what is true about you. I want other people to know how wonderful you are. Help me show them your love and goodness by being good and loving myself. Thank you for sending Jesus to show us what this looks like. I pray these things because I believe in Jesus.

Amen.

List some creative ways you could show and tell others how wonderful God is. Remember, it's not always as simple as telling the story of the Bible. Remember too that you are now God's temple.

....

....

....

....

....

....

Do Something About It

Trace an outline of your left hand on a piece of paper. Then write this verse from Zechariah inside the picture your hand.

> Let your hands be strong so that you can rebuild the temple.
> —ZECHARIAH 8:9

Now trace an outline of your right hand on another piece of paper. The write this verse inside the picture of your hand.

> Don't you know that you yourselves are God's temple? Don't you know that God's Spirit lives among you?
> —1 CORINTHIANS 3:16

Put the drawings of your hands in your room where you will see them. They will remind you to be busy building God's temple.

Week 36, Day 1

Read About It

God will honor anyone who honors him.

What happens when you don't show respect to your parents? Probably nothing good! They deserve your respect. When you show respect to someone, you honor them. And you should show respect both in what you say and in what you do.

That was Malachi's message to God's people. He said they should honor God. But they were having a hard time doing that! They had returned from the land where they had been taken as prisoners. But they felt like God no longer loved them and had given up on them. So, they no longer honored him in their worship or in the way they lived.

The prophet Malachi reminded God's people of God's love for them. Malachi also told them that God had not forgotten them! God was still going to do amazing things. But God's people had to honor God if they wanted to be included in those things! They must trust God because he is worthy of their trust. God knows those who honor him by living this way.

How do you honor people in your life? How do you honor God?

MALACHI

Think About It

The prophet Malachi told God's people to honor God. In this exploration, you'll have to find ways to do that! Find them by searching in the puzzle below. This puzzle is a *sentence* search! The sentences are listed below. They may start out in one direction and then go in another. They might even go in several different directions! The trick is to find the beginning of the sentence. Then trace the sentence in whatever direction it takes! That's how we should honor God. We should do that no matter which direction our life takes!

Search for these ways to honor God in the sentence search puzzle.

HAVE RESPECT FOR HIM.
BE FAITHFUL TO HIM.
BE FAIR WITH ONE ANOTHER.
SHARE WHAT YOU HAVE.
BE HUMBLE.
TRUST HIM.
DO WHAT IS RIGHT AND GOOD.
SERVE HIM.
SPEAK THE TRUTH.
HELP OTHER PEOPLE.
BE PATIENT.
FORGIVE ONE ANOTHER.
BE KIND.

X	F	K	V	A	C	L	H	T	O	J	L	D
H	I	M	O	T	H	P	E	N	N	A	B	C
E	A	D	P	L	E	R	O	P	O	E	N	O
V	O	V	B	E	H	U	M	B	L	E	V	E
R	W	R	E	H	T	O	N	A	E	N	A	V
E	H	Q	F	R	E	S	P	E	C	O	A	I
S	A	T	S	A	I	R	W	I	T	H	U	G
P	I	R	F	H	T	I	A	F	E	B	O	R
E	S	R	U	S	A	H	O	M	P	F	Y	K
A	G	I	L	V	T	R	E	W	H	A	T	B
T	K	H	T	O	H	I	M	T	N	E	I	R
H	E	A	N	I	B	E	K	I	N	D	Y	O
O	T	Q	M	D	G	O	O	D	R	T	U	W
N	R	U	T	H	F	M	L	A	K	G	H	L

223

Week 36, Day 3

Finding Jesus in Malachi

The prophet Malachi reminded God's people that God deserves to be honored. But times were hard for them. They thought God didn't love them anymore. So they stopped honoring God!

We do the same thing. We forget to honor God too! There is only one person who ever lived who honored God all the time. That was Jesus! Sometimes we think life is hard for us. But Jesus had all sorts of really bad things to deal with! People hated him and treated him badly. And then people even crucified him! In spite of all the horrible things that happened to him, Jesus stayed focused on God. Jesus faithfully and perfectly did everything God wanted him to do. By doing that, Jesus honored God.

Use the letters in the word HONOR to think of ways we can honor God. Each word should start with one of the letters in HONOR.

H _____

O _____

N _____

O _____

R _____

Write About It

God's people had a hard time keeping their attention on God. They thought he might have forgotten them. So, they began to forget God! But God never forgets his people. How does it make you feel to know God never forgets about you? Write your thoughts here.

....

....

....

Malachi 3:16–17 says that the Lord knows the names of those who honor him. It also says that when the Lord comes again, those people will be his special treasure! Write how it makes you feel to know you are the Lord's special treasure.

....

....

....

MALACHI

Week 36, Day 5
Pray About It

Dear God,

I want to honor you because you are so worth it! I know that you are coming again. And sometimes waiting for that to happen is hard. While I wait, please help me to live in a way that brings honor to you. Help me to trust you. Help me to treat other people justly. Help me to be willing to give what I have to honor you. And help me to serve you with a willing heart. I ask these things because I believe in Jesus. Amen.

In the grid below, create your own word search using the three words below and three others that help you remember what is important. Challenge a friend or family member to fill in the word search.

Honor
Trust
Justice

....

....

....

	J	U	S	T	I	C	E	
	H	O	N	O	R			
				U				
				S				
				T				

Do Something About It

The message of the prophet Malachi is also for us. The message is that God will honor anyone who honors him. We honor God by the way we live. So, these truths about God should be present in your life.

This exploration will help you remember how to honor God. Make friendship bracelets that you can wear and give to your friends! Find thread, yarn, ribbon, or even colored paper. Then weave or twist the thread, yarn, or ribbon together. Leave enough length so that you can tie it around your wrist. Each color represents a way to honor God. How? By remembering the first letter of the color stands for something specific you can do! Here are possible colors you can use.

After you have made the bracelets, explain to your friends what the colors mean. Every time you see your bracelet it will help you remember to honor God!

Green	=	Giving help to others
Purple	=	Praying to God
Orange	=	Obeying God's instructions
Red	=	Reading the Bible
Yellow	=	Yielding your desires to others
Blue	=	Being your best

Week 37, Day 1

Read About It

Jesus tells us what God's law is all about.

Have you ever looked at something and thought it was something different than what it really was? Maybe you saw a curvy stick in the grass and thought it was a snake. Or maybe you thought a scoop of mashed potatoes was a scoop of ice cream. Some people in the gospel of Matthew were having that problem with the Old Testament law. They thought it was one thing when it was really something else. The people Jesus spoke to thought the law was meant to make their lives hard. They thought it kept them from having a full life. Do this! Don't do that! Who wants to obey all those rules? No one likes it when people tell us what to do. But Jesus said this is the wrong way to think about God's law.

This gospel was written to help them see the truth about the law. You can read about some ways Jesus does this in Matthew 5:21–22, 27–28, 33–34, 38–39, and 43–44. God has given us his law as a gift. Jesus tells us that God's law doesn't keep us from having the best life. In fact, it does just the opposite! It tells us how to have the best life possible! We have the best life when we have a close relationship with God and with one another.

Do you like to be told what to do by a parent or teacher? Do you believe it is because they want you to have the best life?

228

Think About It

The gospel of Matthew shows us that there are good reasons for everything God tells us. We may have thought that God's law was a pain in the neck. But Jesus tells us that it is just the opposite. God's law tells us how to have the best life possible.

Look at each rule below. You may have many of these rules in your life. Draw a line to match each rule to what might happen if you don't follow the it.

1. Put your stuff away when you are finished with it.

a. You might wear it out or break it and cost your parents a lot of money.

2. Don't cross the street without looking both ways.

b. Someone might trip on something that was left out.

c. You could accidentally hurt someone.

3. Play gently with others.

4. Don't wear flip-flops while riding a bike.

d. You may wake up crabby and have a hard time learning.

5. Don't jump on the furniture.

e. Your feet can get caught and you might fall.

6. Go to bed on time.

f. You could be hit by a car.

229

Week 37, Day 3

Finding Jesus in Matthew

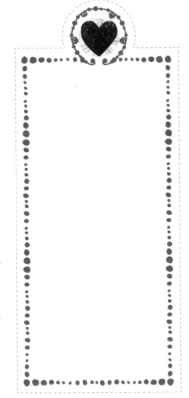

God gave the law to his people to tell them how to live the best life possible. But most people thought God's law was only a list of rules. They thought it kept a person from having fun. But Jesus taught them about all the benefits that come from following God's law. But none of us live exactly as God tells us to in the law. Sin has messed us up. Sin keeps us from doing what we know are the right things to do. Jesus perfectly follows God's law for us. Now because of Jesus, all the benefits of following God's law come to anyone who believes in him! Something else happens, too, when we believe in Jesus. He sends his Holy Spirit to us! The Holy Spirit helps us to become more and more like Jesus. That's what God has always wanted for us. That's why he gave us his law in the first place!

Create a bookmark to keep your place as you read the book of Matthew. Use it to remind yourself of God's most important rule. Write the verse below on your bookmark.

Love the Lord your God with all your heart and with all your soul. Love him with all your mind. ... This is the first and most important commandment.

—MATTHEW 22:37–38

Week 37, Day 4
Write About It

Jesus explained why God gave us his law. God gave it to show us how to have the best life possible. Has learning this changed how you think about the rules God has given us? Write your thoughts below.

....

....

....

When we believe in Jesus, he sends his Holy Spirit to us. The Holy Spirit helps us follow God's law just as Jesus did. Then we will have the best life possible. What parts of God's law do you find the most difficult? What can you ask the Holy Spirit to help you with? Write your thoughts below.

....

....

....

Pray About It

Dear God,

Thank you for giving me your law. It shows me how I can have the full life you want for me. Thank you that Jesus has perfectly obeyed your law for me. Now I know that I will always have your blessing. Thank you, too, for sending the Holy Spirit to me. I want the Spirit to help me follow your law just as Jesus did. Then I'll have the blessings you want me to have. I ask you for these things because I believe in Jesus. Amen.

How can you do the things Jesus talks about in the following verses? Write some ideas.

Matthew 5:16—Let your light shine so others can see it.

....

....

Matthew 5:22—Do not be angry with a brother or sister.

....

....

232

Matthew 5:39—Do not fight against an evil person.

....

....

Matthew 5:44—Pray for those who hurt you.

....

....

Matthew 6:14—Forgive other people when they sin against you.

....

....

Matthew 6:25—Do not worry.

....

....

Matthew 7:1—Do not judge other people.

....

....

Week 37, Day 6

Do Something About It

This exploration will remind you of Matthew's message. It shows how the true meaning of something can get lost. That's what happened to the people in Matthew's gospel. Over time, people had forgotten why God had given them the law. They no longer understood its true meaning. Now you'll get to see how that can happen!

Get five or more people together for the game. Sit in a circle or a straight line. You can be the first person. Whisper a message to the person next to you. Make sure no one else hears! Here is what you should whisper. "The shy short shepherd's sixth sheep was so sick since she swallowed seven shrimps." Then have the second person whisper the message they heard to the third person. Keep going from one person to the next until you get to the last person. Have the last person repeat the message they heard. (It probably won't sound anything like the original!)

This happened to God's people in the gospel of Matthew. Over time the message that God's law was good had become mixed up. In fact, by Jesus' time the people thought the law was something bad. They needed to be shown that they had received the wrong message!

Read About It

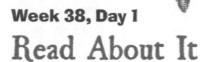

MARK

Jesus suffered for our sake.

No one likes it when bad things happen to them. Many times these bad things happen because of things we've done. For example, you might have received a low grade on a test because you didn't study. Or maybe you didn't get to eat dessert because you didn't eat all your dinner. Those are certainly not things you enjoy! But you can understand why they happen. You did something wrong, and bad things resulted.

You know what would be even worse? Suppose you hadn't done anything wrong at all and bad things happened to you anyway! That wouldn't seem fair! Suppose you did study hard for the test and failed anyway! Suppose you did eat all your dinner but still didn't get any dessert! You'd probably be pretty upset! That's how it was for the people that Mark was writing to in his gospel. The Romans were giving Christians a really hard time. The Christians hadn't done anything wrong, but that didn't matter to the Romans. They were treating the Christians badly. They were even killing some of them! The Christians were upset and confused. They thought that if they believed in Jesus, they would have a wonderful life. But their lives were not wonderful. In fact, they were really suffering! Mark encouraged these suffering believers by reminding them about Jesus.

Has anyone given you a hard time because you were a Christian? How did it feel? What did you do about it?

Week 38, Day 2

Think About It

Mark reminded believers that something good can come from something bad. This exploration will remind you of that. Read the short story below. Remove the things in each line that are listed on the right side. When you're done, read the story again with the words that remain. You'll find that what began as something bad ended up as something good!

WORDS TO REMOVE
(be careful to remove the commas and periods, too, if they are shown below!)

Jamie had a puppy named Floppy. Jamie loved Floppy and he loved Jamie. One day Jamie took Floppy for a walk. It was a nice day in the park. And when Floppy saw a squirrel, he ran after it. The squirrel ran a long way and so did Floppy! After a while, Floppy gave up chasing the squirrel and decided it was time he came back to Jamie. He thought he knew how to get back to her, but he didn't. Then Jamie walked all over with sadness looking for Floppy. She looked all that day but didn't find him. All her neighbors knew Floppy. And they would have loved to help, but they hadn't seen Floppy either. Jamie was not happy at all. She wanted so much for Floppy to find his way back to her. She looked for him every day. Jamie was afraid that she might never be able to see and play with Floppy again.

decided it was time
he thought he
, but he didn't
sadness looking
for . She looked but didn't
find him Floppy.
they would have to help, but they hadn't
seen either not at
all for Floppy to find
his way back to her. She looked for him
. Jamie was afraid that she might never
able

Finding Jesus in Mark

Mark reminds believers that if anyone didn't deserve to suffer, it was Jesus. But Mark reminds believers that God used Jesus' suffering to accomplish some truly wonderful things. Here is what Jesus says in Mark 10:45. "Even the Son of Man did not come to be served. Instead, he came to serve others. He came to give his life as the price for setting many people free."

Mark 10:45 is a great verse to memorize. Look at how this verse is broken up below. Draw a picture in the box for each line to help you remember this verse.

Even the Son of Man

did not come to be served.

Instead,

he came to serve others.

He came to give his life

237

as the price for setting many people free.

Write About It

Jesus never did anything wrong. But people did all sorts of evil things to him. Write how you think Jesus must have felt when that happened to him. Choose a color from Hearty's color chart on page 7 that represents these feelings. Use the color you chose to color lightly over the words you wrote.

....

....

....

Jesus knew that because of his suffering and death many people would be saved. God tells us he can use the bad things that happen to us to accomplish good things too. How does knowing this make you feel about the bad things that happen to you? Write your thoughts below.

....

....

....

Week 38, Day 5

Pray About It

Dear God,

Thank you for Jesus. He was so good even though people were so mean to him! I can't imagine how this made him feel. It's amazing that Jesus would give his life to save mine. You are in control of all things. So when bad things happen to me, you're doing something good through them too. Help me to be like Jesus when those bad things happen. Help me to be willing to go through them to help other people. Help me do this even when I don't understand how it will help them. I ask you for these things because I believe in Jesus. Amen.

God can even use hard times to do good things. Think of as many words as you can that mean the same thing as GOOD. Write them on the lines below.

Week 38, Day 6

Do Something About It

It can be hard to remember that God is at work in both good times and bad times. This week when something bad happens, think about something good it could cause. It might not be easy to do. You might have to think for a while! For example, you might be sad because the rain ruined a field trip. But that rain might have been needed by a farmer growing crops.

Do this for at least five things. You can use the chart below to keep a record.

Something Bad that Happened	Something Good that Could Result

Read About It

**Jesus came to seek and to
save what was lost.**

Everybody gets sick. If it's bad enough, you go to the doctor. If you take medicine, you can become healthy again! But suppose you don't want to take medicine. Then you could become even sicker! So why wouldn't you take the medicine and be cured?

Sin is a sickness too. But it's a spiritual sickness instead of a physical one. Luke was a doctor, and he talks about the sickness of sin. He says sin has infected everyone and no one can escape it. That means no one's relationship with God is perfectly healthy! But often people don't know they are infected by sin. Or maybe they don't want to know. But as with any other sickness, ignoring sin won't make it go away.

Luke tells us that there is a cure for sin. The cure is Jesus! But before we can ask for the cure, we have to admit that we're sick! In Luke 5:31–32 Jesus said that healthy people don't need a doctor. Sick people do. When we admit that sin has infected us, we can turn to Jesus for the cure. When we believe in him, he cures our sin. Then our broken relationship with God is healed.

Why do you think some people won't let Jesus heal their broken relationship with God?

241

Think About It

Each line in the activity below has several words in it. Only one of the words in each line is found in a sentence in Luke 19:10. When you think you have found the word, put a circle around it. Then write it on the lines below. When you have the right words, the sentence will tell you what Jesus came to do.

1. thethenthattasktturnstake (3 letters)
2. servesavesongsonsuresoup (3 letters)
3. adgotoofmymeman (2 letters)
4. moomarkmassmanmore (3 letters)
5. camecorecratecraft (4 letters)
6. onoveruptoinatmake (2 letters)
7. lamelakeslooklastlives (4 letters)
8. foldfactfunfumefor (3 letters)
9. thatthethistherethose (3 letters)
10. lostlastleastliveleftlead (4 letters)
11. awayactaddandaidealso (3 letters)
12. sicksadsupersavesacksink (4 letters)
13. thosethesethemtheirthisthat (4 letters)

___ ___ ___ ___ ___ ___

___ ___ ___ ___

242

Finding Jesus in Luke

What Luke wanted us to know about Jesus is clear. Jesus is the cure for sin! That's because Jesus was the only human being who wasn't infected by sin. So only Jesus could seek out sin and save people from it. Jesus died to provide the final cure for sin. And his cure is so effective not even death has power over him! And death has no power over those who believe in him either!

When we believe in Jesus, he makes us spiritually healthy again! And Jesus brings his cure for sin into every part of our lives. He brings it to our thoughts, our feelings, and our actions. Anyone who believes in Jesus will receive this cure for their sin. Our relationships with God and with one another can be healthy again. All we have to do is ask Jesus for the cure!

Think of some things that need to be cured in your life. Write these things on the lines next to Hearty's doctor bag. These are all the things that Jesus will cure in your life.

243

Week 39, Day 4

Write About It

Jesus came to save people from the sickness of sin. It doesn't matter who you are or what you've done! When you are sorry for your sin and believe in Jesus, he will cure you! Then you will have a healthy relationship with God again! Write how knowing this makes you feel.

....

....

....

....

Luke 15:10 says, "There is joy in heaven over one sinner who turns away from sin." That happens when a person believes in Jesus and receives the cure for their sin. They're spiritually healthy again. There's a celebration in heaven! Write how knowing that makes you feel.

....

....

....

....

Week 39, Day 5

Pray About It

Dear God,

You are so great and powerful. You have power and authority over everything. Thank you that your son, Jesus, came to seek and to save what was lost. He gave his life to provide a cure for my sin and to give me new life. Thank you so much for saving me and giving me that new life. Now I know that my relationship with you is healthy again! I pray this because I believe in Jesus.
Amen.

Study the words from Luke 5:31–32. Try to memorize these words that Jesus said. Maybe put the words to music. Or write the words over and over to help you remember them.

"Healthy people don't need a doctor. Sick people do. I have not come to get those who think they are right with God to follow me. I have come to get sinners to turn away from their sins."

245

Week 39, Day 6

Do Something About It

Jesus came to seek and to save what was lost! This activity is a treasure hunt that you will design. You will be the guide and give the clues. First you need to make the treasure. Write Luke 19:10 (written below) on a piece of paper. Wrap this paper around your favorite piece of candy or other fun surprise. Decide where you'll hide the treasure. Put it there while no one is looking.

Now make a map for each treasure hunter. The map should have at least five clues to solve before the treasure can be found. The clues should lead the treasure hunters to several places indoors and outdoors. Include at least one place that's hard to get to.

The hunt is over when someone finds the treasure. That person gets to read the verse and keep the treasure. But then celebrate with everybody. The celebration will remind you of the celebration in heaven when someone finds Jesus.

"The Son of Man came to look for the lost and save them."
—Luke 19:10

Read About It

JOHN

Jesus is both God and a human being.

Have you ever wondered if one thing can be something else at the same time? Can a bench be a seat and also a table? Could your sister be your sister and also a daughter? Of course! It's also true that Jesus is both God and a human being at the same time! Did you ever really think about that? Well, the apostle John did! He wrote this book to tell us more about it.

John begins his gospel by telling us that Jesus was present at creation. Only God was present at creation so Jesus must be God! And because he's God, Jesus is the source of all life. The miracles he performed show us this. Jesus healed sick people and even raised his friend, Lazarus, from the dead!

At the same time, Jesus is also a human being. He was born to parents. He ate food and celebrated the holidays with his disciples. But Jesus is the only human being who didn't sin. Because he didn't sin, he could pay the price for everyone who does.

Jesus gave up his life to pay for our sins so that we could have life. Jesus had to be both God and a human being to do this. Everyone who believes in him can have as close a relationship with God as Jesus has!

Are you one thing and also something else? What are they? Explain.

247

Week 40, Day 2

Think About It

In the gospel of John, we learn that Jesus is two things at the same time.

There are two words given at the beginning of each sentence below. These words are examples of things that can be two things at the same time. These two words are somewhere in the sentence that follows them. When you find the two words, underline or highlight them. You'll have to search because they might be parts of other words.

brother/son	Hey bro, the room is on fire!
mother/wife	She sold him other flowers for his wife.
star/sun	He never spreads his tar on Sunday.
sister/friend	My sis terrifies her friendships.
parent/teacher	Apparently, the feet of Kate ache really badly.
dirt/mud	His dirty hands smudged the window.
tomato/fruit	I saw Tom at one of the fruit stands.
seat/chair	By the sea, the beach air was salty.
dad/farmer	He purchased a dog from a far merchant.

Week 40, Day 3

Finding Jesus in John

The apostle John wants us to know that Jesus is both God and a human being. Jesus has to be both if he is going to be able to save us. Jesus has to be a human being so that he can represent us human beings. Jesus paid the price for our sin. He did that even though he never sinned. He did that because he loves us so much!

Jesus also has to be God. If he weren't, he'd have to pay for his own sins. But because he's God, he has no sin. After Jesus paid for our sin, he sent his Holy Spirit. He sent his Holy Spirit to everyone who believes in him. The Holy Spirit helps us to have an even closer relationship with God. Here is what Jesus said in John 10:10 about everyone who believes in him. "I have come so they may have life. I want them to have it in the fullest possible way." What a wonderful gift Jesus gives to us!

Color the illustrations below to help you remember God, his Son, and the Holy Spirit.

God the
Father

God the
Son

God the
Holy Spirit

249

Write About It

Do you believe that Jesus is both God and human? Even Jesus' disciples had a hard time believing it. Jesus tells them in John 10:30, "I and the Father are one." Think about this verse. Then write how it helps you believe Jesus is both God and a human being.

....

....

....

....

Jesus is both God and a human being. He makes it possible for believers to have a relationship with God. When you believe in Jesus, you have a relationship with God too! Write how that makes you feel.

....

....

....

....

Week 40, Day 5

Pray About It

Dear God,

I know that Jesus is both God and a human being. But I don't understand it very well. Please help me to trust and believe even when I don't understand very well. I believe that Jesus died to pay for my sins. By doing that, Jesus made it possible for me to have a relationship with you. Thank you for that relationship. And thank you for sending your Holy Spirit to help me do what is right. Please help me to have a closer relationship with you. I pray these things because I believe in Jesus.

Amen.

Use this chart to help you remember Jesus as God and Jesus as a human being. Write key words from what you've learned this week in each column.

Jesus as God	Jesus as Human Being

251

Do Something About It

Jesus is both God and a human being. When you believe in Jesus, you also have a relationship with the Father. And Jesus sends his Holy Spirit to help you do what is right.

Now it's time to do some art! Follow the directions below to learn something important about God.

In the letters of GOD below, the G contains the first two letters of FATHER. It contains the first letter of SON. And it contains the first three letters of HOLY SPIRIT. Look in the other parts of GOD to find the other letters.

Color in the letters for FATHER, SON, and HOLY SPIRIT with different colors. Use a different color for each word. When you have colored all the letters, the picture will remind you of something true about God. It will remind you that the Father, Son, and Holy Spirit are all God.

252

Read About It

God makes his church powerful and bigger through the work of the Holy Spirit.

Have you ever stood in the wind? You can feel it blow through your hair. You can see it send dust swirling down the street. But you can't actually see the wind. You can only experience it and see what it does.

Just as you can't see the wind, you can't see the Holy Spirit. But you can experience the presence of the Holy Spirit in your life. And you can see proof of the Holy Spirit at work building the church. That was just as true for Jesus' disciples as it is for all believers today. The book of Acts tells us that Jesus sent his Holy Spirit to his disciples. It happened while they were in Jerusalem. The Holy Spirit came to them with the sound of a strong wind. Then they began to tell other people about the good news of new life in Jesus. The apostles Peter and Paul led the church in telling people about Jesus. As a result, many other people believed in Jesus Christ.

The Holy Spirit continues to do his work today. He gives believers courage and power. Then they can tell other people about the good news of new life in Jesus. And when believers do this, the number of believers continues to grow!

Are you telling other people about the good news of new life in Jesus? How is the Holy Spirit giving you courage and power to do this?

253

Week 41, Day 2
Think About It

Something was happening in the church. The message about Jesus was spreading! What was causing this to happen? You can find the answer by solving this puzzle! Unscramble the words for each clue. When you're done unscrambling the words, write down all the circled letters. Then unscramble the circled letters.

WERPO
"You will receive ⬜⬜⬜⬜⬜."
Read Acts 1:8 for a clue.

WIGBLON
"It was like a strong wind ⬜⬜⬜⬜⬜⬜."
Read Acts 2:2 for a clue.

HOPESPYR
Your sons and daughters will ⬜⬜⬜⬜⬜⬜⬜⬜.
Read Acts 2:17 for a clue.

DBLO
"They were ⬜⬜⬜⬜ when they spoke God's word."
Read Acts 4:31 for a clue.

FIGT
Some believers "were amazed" because this ⬜⬜⬜⬜
"had been poured out even on the Gentiles."
Read Acts 10:45 for a clue.

254

Unscramble the circled letters here.

—— —— —— —— —— —— —— —— ——

Week 41, Day 3

Finding Jesus in Acts

Jesus came to do the will of God the Father. Jesus began this work while he was on earth. He taught other people that he was God's son. Jesus showed his power and authority to forgive sin and bring life. Before Jesus went up to heaven, he gave his disciples a command. In Matthew 28:19 he told them they should "go and make disciples of all nations." After Jesus went up to heaven, he sent his Holy Spirit to his disciples. The Holy Spirit guided and encouraged them in this work. So the disciples had courage to tell many other people the good news about Jesus.

But that's not something that only the first disciples should do. That's something everyone who believes in Jesus should do! Whenever someone believes in Jesus, the Holy Spirit comes to them too.

Jesus talked about the disciples catching believers like they caught fish. Color the drawing below and hang it in your room. Remember to pray for others so that they will believe in Jesus too.

ACTS

Write About It

When Jesus went up to heaven, he gave his disciples a task. Jesus told them to tell other people about him. When you believe in Jesus, you are given the same task. You should tell other people the good news about Jesus. How do you feel about doing that task? Write your thoughts here.

....

....

....

....

....

The Holy Spirit has come to you to guide and encourage you in that task. The Spirit helps you to have courage to tell other people the good news about Jesus. Does knowing God's Holy Spirit is helping you make you feel better about doing that task? Write your thoughts here.

....

....

....

....

....

Pray About It

Dear God,

Sometimes I wish I could see the Holy Spirit! But the wind can remind me of your Spirit's presence. When it blows all around me, I'll remember that your Holy Spirit is with me! Thank you for sending your Holy Spirit to me. I love knowing you are with me and guiding me. Please help me to have courage. Help me to be ready to tell other people the good news about Jesus. I want the whole world to know about it! I pray this because I believe in Jesus.
Amen.

Create a wind catcher or chime and hang it where you see it often. It will help you remember the Holy Spirit.

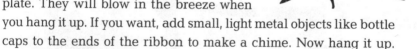

Decorate a paper plate. Attach crepe paper strips or ribbons to the edges of the plate. They will blow in the breeze when you hang it up. If you want, add small, light metal objects like bottle caps to the ends of the ribbon to make a chime. Now hang it up. When you hear or see it blow in the wind, you will be reminded of the Holy Spirit.

257

ACTS

Do Something About It

The Holy Spirit came first to the church in Jerusalem. But the Spirit didn't just stay there! The good news about new life in Jesus spread throughout the whole world!

This adventure will help you to see what was going on. First, find a map of the apostle Paul's missionary journeys. Most Bibles have a map section in the back. On that map find the cities of Jerusalem, Antioch, Ephesus, Corinth, Athens, and Rome. Lay a thin piece of paper over the map and mark the locations of these cities on the paper.

Find a flat surface that's okay for you to get paint on or get wet. Lay your paper on it. Then put two or three drops of food coloring in a glass of water. Use a straw to stir it around. Carefully drop a small amount of the colored water on the word "Jerusalem." Use the straw to blow the colored water toward Antioch and all the other cities. You may have to add more colored water at the Jerusalem location. Continue to do this until the colored water is spread to all the cities.

Your blowing through the straw is like the wind of the Holy Spirit! You can't see the air moving but you can see what it does. The colored water is like the good news of new life in Jesus. You can see it spread as a result of the work of the Holy Spirit.

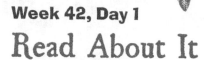

Week 42, Day 1

Read About It

God brings everyone who believes in Jesus from death to life.

Have you ever had a pet that died? You were probably very sad! But being sad couldn't bring your pet back to life. When something is dead, it won't live again. But there is an exception! And Paul writes about this exception in his letter to believers in Rome.

Paul begins his letter by talking about sin. He says everybody has sinned, and that sin is worthy of God's judgment of death. In fact, people controlled by sin are already spiritually dead. Whew! That's heavy stuff we don't like to hear about even though we need to! But Paul goes on to say that God has provided a way out. When anyone puts their faith in Jesus, their sins are forgiven. Because of their faith in Jesus, God gives them a new life. They are no longer spiritually dead! They are spiritually alive! Their old life that was controlled by sin is gone.

The apostle Paul has instructions for these new believers. Here is what he says in Romans 6:13. "You have been brought from death to life. So give every part of yourself to God to do what is right." Paul wanted these new believers to work at having a closer relationship with God. As they did that, they would become more like Jesus in the way they lived. Paul wrote to the believers in Rome. But his words are for us as well!

When you believe in Jesus, you are no longer spiritually dead. You're spiritually alive! How does that make you feel?

259

Think About It

God brings everyone who believes in Jesus from death to life. Here is a puzzle to help you remember this wonderful truth. The words "Dead" and "Life" are written below. You have to figure out how to get from the word "dead" to the word "life." But it's not so easy! You may only change one letter at a time to do it. It will take you several steps. The first step has been done for you to help you get started.

DEAD

LEAD

_ _ _ _

_ _ _ _

_ _ _ _

_ _ _ _

_ _ _ _

LIFE

Finding Jesus in Romans

The beginning of the book of Romans is hard to read. It talks about all the bad things sin has done to us. The apostle Paul says that all of us are already spiritually dead. And we still have to face God's judgment for our sin. It all seems so hopeless!

But God himself has provided an answer to this hopeless situation. God has sent Jesus to pay the price for our sins. Isn't it amazing that Jesus was willing to do this for us! When we believe in Jesus, two wonderful things happen. First, we don't have to worry anymore about God's judgment against our sin. And second, Jesus makes us spiritually alive again by sending his Holy Spirit to us. The Holy Spirit is making us become more and more like Jesus. So everything we say and do will look more like what Jesus said and did. As that happens, our spiritual life will become stronger and stronger. We'll be experiencing more of the wonderful life God wants us to have.

Here is something to help you remember the most important message of Romans. Copy the verse below onto an index card. Decorate it and use it as your bookmark for the book of Romans.

We are made right with God by putting our faith in Jesus Christ. This happens to all who believe.
—Romans 3:22

ROMANS

Week 42, Day 4

Write About It

When you believe in Jesus, you have new life! Jesus sends his Holy Spirit to live with you and guide you. How does it make you feel to know that God does this for you?

....

....

....

....

....

The apostle Paul wants believers to have the best new life possible. That life comes when we live like Jesus. What does it look like to live like Jesus? In Romans 12:9–21, Paul describes many ways to be like Christ. Read these verses and then write five ways you can be like Jesus.

....

....

....

....

262

Week 42, Day 5

Pray About It

Dear God,

Thank you for sending your son, Jesus. I know he died so that I could live. I know that Jesus paid for my sins because I couldn't do it. I'm not perfect, but he is. Thank you for sending your Holy Spirit to me. I ask that your Holy Spirit guide me in living this new life you've given me. I want to be loving and caring. And I want to serve you. Please help me to be like Jesus. I know that now I will never die but live with you forever. And I'm sure of this because I believe in Jesus. Amen.

Draw the outline of a cross on wax paper. Use crayons or permanent markers to color in the sections to create a stained-glass cross. Hang the cross where the sun can shine on it. It will remind you of what Jesus has done for you.

HELLO! NICE TO MEET YOU!

Week 42, Day 6

Do Something About It

When you believe in Jesus, you want to live so others see your new life. In Romans 12, Paul describes what that life looks like. It is a life that shows other people that you are guided by the Holy Spirit. You will live showing love for other people and serving them. Read Romans 12. Each verse tells you how you should live your new life. Find key words to help you. Then write a plan for how you will live showing each one in your life. We've done one example for you.

What I Should Do	What I Will Do
Love	I will write a kind note to my classmate who is being bullied.

Read About It

**God gives gifts to his people
so that they can give too.**

Everybody likes to receive gifts. But what if we always expected gifts? What if we didn't even think of them as gifts anymore? What if we thought we had a right to them? What if everyone wanted to be given things but nobody wanted to be the giver? There's no way that could work!

In 1 & 2 Corinthians, the apostle Paul is writing to Christians who are having problems. They don't understand what giving is all about. They don't understand why the Holy Spirit has given them spiritual gifts. They think they have been given those gifts to enjoy for themselves. They all want to get those gifts from God. But nobody wants to use them to give help to anyone else! In 1 Corinthians 3:2 Paul says they are acting like babies!

But the apostle Paul tells us why God gives us gifts. And it's not just so that we can enjoy them for ourselves. In 2 Corinthians 9:11, Paul tells us why God gives us so many things. "You will be made rich in every way. Then you can always give freely." That means that God gives to us so that we can give to others. When we live like that, we'll become more and more like Jesus!

What does it feel like to receive a gift you really like? What does it feel like to give something to someone?

1 & 2 CORINTHIANS

Week 43, Day 2

Think About It

Giving to other people makes us more like Jesus. If we can give just one thing to someone else, we can make their lives better. This exploration will remind you of that. Give these words one or more letters to make them into something better. You can add the letters at the beginning, the middle, or the end. For example, the word "rust" isn't very good. Things that aren't well cared for rust. But if you give the word an extra letter "t" at the beginning you end up with "trust." See if you can help out the rest of these words by giving them one or more letters. Write the new word in the blank after each word. There are all sorts of possibilities!

1. hot _____

2. mean _____

3. break _____

4. ow _____

5. dim _____

6. bad _____

7. ban _____

8. sin _____

9. war _____

10. we _____

11. not _____

12. heat _____

13. tar _____

14. hard _____

15. end _____

Finding Jesus in 1 & 2 Corinthians

The apostle Paul writes to the believers in the city of Corinth about something very important. He's writing to them about giving. That's because Jesus was all about giving! Jesus gave everything he had to help other people. He didn't demand anything for himself. He even gave his life for us! By giving his life for us, Jesus gave everyone who believes in him eternal life. And even then, he still wasn't done giving! After he went to heaven, Jesus sent his Holy Spirit to believers.

The Holy Spirit helps believers become better at giving, just like Jesus. People who are becoming more like Jesus know that real joy comes from giving. And God wants us to have real joy. That's why he gives so much to us. He does that so we'll have plenty to give to other people. And God wants us to have the joy of giving to other people!

There are lots of ways you can give to people. You can spend time with them. You can do something for them. You can help them in other ways. Every time you give something to someone, draw an apple on the tree below. When your tree is full, your heart will be full, too!

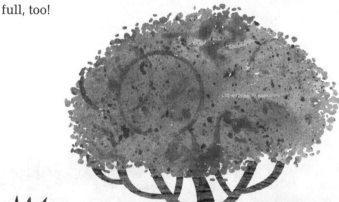

267

1 & 2 CORINTHIANS

Week 43, Day 4

Write About It

Think about all the gifts that God has given to you. Look up these verses. Then write down what they say God has given to anyone who believes in Jesus Christ.

John 1:12 _____

John 3:16 _____

1 Corinthians 12:7 _____

2 Peter 1:3 _____

1 John 5:11 _____

The apostle Paul says believers who don't give are like babies. Babies only take. But believers who give to help other people are like Jesus. Are you more like a baby or like Jesus? Write your thoughts here.

....

....

Pray About It

Dear God,

You have given me so many wonderful things. You have given me eternal life when I believed in Jesus. You have given me your Holy Spirit. You have given me special abilities to help other people. But I haven't always done that. I want to be more like Jesus. He gave everything to help other people. So I want to give more too. Please show me ways I can do that. I ask you for these things because I believe in Jesus.
Amen.

The Holy Spirit will show you how to use your abilities to help other people. When you think of ways to give more like Jesus, write them on the signs below.

1 & 2 CORINTHIANS

Do Something About It

There are all sorts of things you can give to other people to help them. You can give the gift of your time or your money. You can give the gift of your care, your work, or your prayer. And the gift doesn't have to be big to have a big effect. Sometimes just doing something little for someone else can mean a lot to them. You can probably think of many things you could do to help other people. But here is one easy thing you can do that anyone would be thankful for.

Think of someone you know who is having a hard time. Make a card for them to let them know that you are praying for them. Let them know that you care for them and that they are not alone. Make a drawing of your card below. Then make the real card out of colored paper. Have one of your parents or another adult help you find their address and mail your card. That might be all it takes to help that person get through their problems. Just imagine how happy they'll be to get your card! The joy you give them will give you joy too! And you will be become more like Jesus!

270

Read About It

God wants us to trust him and not ourselves for our salvation.

Can you scoop ice cream with a wet noodle? Of course, you can't! That's because a wet noodle wasn't made to scoop ice cream. Trying to do something with the wrong tool just won't work.

The Galatians were believers who were trying to use God's law for the wrong purpose. They thought it could do something it was never meant to do. They thought it could give them eternal life if they obeyed it! They thought that by keeping the law, they could be made right with God. But the apostle Paul tells them that they were very, very wrong! Here is what he says at the end of Galatians 2:16. "No one can be made right with God by obeying the law." And why is that? Because only by perfectly obeying God's law could anyone earn eternal life. But the problem is that none of us can perfectly obey God's law! The only person who can perfectly obey is Jesus. We need to trust Jesus to save us and not our own efforts. That's because our own efforts could never be good enough. God's law describes how to live the life God wants for us. But it doesn't give us that life. We can only get that life by believing in Jesus.

How does knowing you need to trust in Jesus to have your best life make you feel?

271

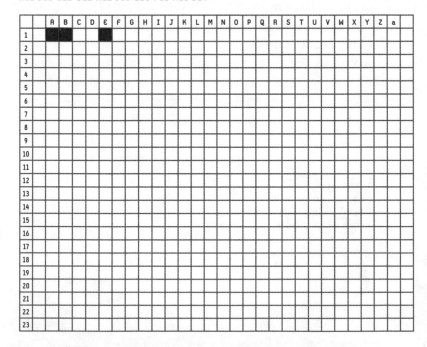

GALATIANS

Week 44, Day 2

Think About It

Help the Galatians find the correct way to become right with God! Color in the squares to see the apostle Paul's message. Find the letter and number provided for each clue. Color in the square where the letter and number meet. The first three are done for you to show you how to do it.

A1 B1 E1 F1 G1 I1 M1 O1 P1 Q1 S1 W1 Y1
Z1 a1 A2 C2 E2 I2 M2 O2 S2 W2 Y2 A3 C3
E3 I3 M3 O3 S3 W3 Y3
A4 B4 E4 F4 I4 M4 O4 P4 S4 W4 Y4 Z4 A5
C5 E5 I5 M5 O5 S5 W5 Y5 A6 C6 E6 I6 M6
O6 T6 V6 Y6 A7 B7 E7
F7 G7 I7 J7 K7 M7 O7 P7 Q7 U7 Y7 Z7 a7
J9 L9 R9 J10 L10 M10 R10 J11 L11 N11
R11 J12 L12 O12 R12 J13 L13 P13 R13 J14

L14 Q14 R14 J15 L15 R15 F17 H17 I17 J17
M17 N17 Q17 T17 W17 X17 F18 H18 L18 O18
Q18 T18 V18 Y18 F19
H19 L19 Q19 T19 V19 F20 H20 I20 M20
N20 Q20 T20 W20 X20 F21 H21 O21 Q21
T21 Y21 C22 F22 H22 L22 O22
Q22 T22 V22 Y22 D23 E23 H23 I23 J23
M23 N23 R23 S23 W23 X23

272

Finding Jesus in Galatians

When we look for Jesus in Galatians, we're doing what the Galatians themselves forgot to do! They forgot about what Jesus had done for them. And they were trying to do it themselves!

Jesus perfectly obeyed all of God's laws for us. So when we believe in Jesus, God gives us credit for what Jesus did! Isn't that amazing! Why would anyone try to do something impossible when Jesus has already done it for us? Here is what Paul says in Galatians 2:16: "Here is what we know. No one is made right with God by obeying the law. It is by believing in Jesus Christ."

Believers still try to follow God's instructions. But we don't do that to try to be right with God. We follow God's instructions because doing that will make us more like Jesus.

This verse will remind you of your place in God's kingdom. Copy Galatians 2:20 below. Decorate it. Then hang it in your room.

I have been crucified with Christ. I don't live any longer, but Christ lives in me. Now I live my life in my body by faith in the Son of God. He loved me and gave himself for me.
—GALATIANS 2:20

Week 44, Day 4

Write About It

Have you ever felt like you had to earn God's blessing? Do you have a hard time believing there is nothing you can do to earn your salvation? Write your thoughts below.

....

....

....

Think about what it would be like if you had to earn your salvation. How well do you think you would be able to obey all of God's law? How does this make you more thankful for what Jesus has done for you? Write your thoughts below.

....

....

....

Week 44, Day 5

Pray About It

Dear God,

I admit that sometimes I think I can earn your blessing. I think that by being good and obeying your law I earn points with you. But I know that's not true. I have all the points I need because of Jesus Christ. I know that he is the only one who could ever perfectly obey your law. Thank you for giving me credit for what he has done. Please help me to trust him and not myself for my salvation. I ask you for these things because I believe in Jesus.

Amen.

Cut out the bookmark here. Use it to keep track of your progress through the book of Galatians.

No one is made **right** with God by **obeying** the law. It is by **believing** in Jesus Christ. So we too have put our **faith** in Christ Jesus.

—Galatians 2:16

Do Something About It

The Galatians were trying to use something for the wrong purpose. They were trying to use God's law as a way to be saved. But the only way to be saved is by believing in Jesus. This exploration will help you remember the mistake of the Galatians. That's because you'll be trying to use something for the wrong purpose too!

You need at least two players for this game. Each player should have a golf ball and a plastic straw. Play this game outside on the grass or inside on carpet. First set up a starting line. Then set up a finish line about 15 to 20 feet away. This is your golf course. If you're really creative, you can make the course larger and more difficult!

When you have your course set up, place everyone's golf balls along the starting line. Each player uses their plastic straw as a golf club. They must try to move their golf ball from the starting line to the finish line. Players have to take turns hitting their ball with their straws. They may only hit their ball one time each turn. The player who gets their golf ball to the finish line first wins!

Remember, the Galatians were trying to be saved by trusting in what *they* did instead of what *God* did. They had to remember that they needed to trust God and not themselves for their salvation.

Read About It

**God uses his people to show what he
wants human beings to be like.**

EPHESIANS

Has something ever stopped working for you the way it
was supposed to? Maybe your bike got a flat tire. Maybe
the zipper stuck on your backpack or your shoelace broke. You just
want things to work like they should! Sin keeps us from working the
way we're supposed to. That's why God sent Jesus Christ.

The apostle Paul wrote this letter to the church in Ephesus. He
wanted these believers to know that God fixes what sin has broken.
They now have new life in Jesus Christ. But they can't just keep it
for themselves. Paul reminds them that they must show that new life
to other people. And they are to do that in the way they live with
one another.

What Paul wrote to the believers in Ephesus is also true for us.
When we believe in Jesus Christ, God makes us whole again. We
too have that wonderful, new life God wants for us. And we also
must show other people what that life in Jesus Christ looks like.
We must show that new life in the way we treat other believers.
And we must show that new life to everyone in our lives.

**Have you ever felt that things in your life aren't working the
way they are supposed to? What can you do to change that?**

Think About It

Paul tells us what the good life looks like. Look up the verses below. Notice what Paul does. He first describes one way sin has broken us. Then he describes the way God makes us whole again. Find the opposite way to live that God makes possible for us.

Ephesians 4:25   Instead of lying, we _____

Ephesians 4:28   Instead of stealing, we _____

Ephesians 4:29   Instead of evil talk, we _____

Ephesians 4:31–32 Instead of hatred, we should _____

When we do these good things, people can hear and see them. When they do, they'll understand the kind of life God wants for them too. It's the life they can have by believing in Jesus.

Finding Jesus in Ephesians

So what does believing in Jesus Christ have to do with becoming whole again? The apostle Paul tells us that before we believed in Jesus Christ, we were broken. Read Ephesians 2:12. In that verse, Paul tells how we were before we believed in Jesus. It's not a pretty picture! He says we were without hope and without God. But that's not how God created us to be. God wants so much more for us than that!

Now read Ephesians 2:17–19. Did you catch all the good things that are true for anyone who believes in Jesus? We have peace. We are no longer outsiders and strangers to God. We are citizens of God's kingdom. We are members of God's family! Those are all amazing things! And they are all things that Jesus does for us when we believe in him.

We are all members of God's family! Write the names of the people in your Christian life on small pieces of paper. Glue these names on the tree below. Remember, "You are citizens together with God's people. You are also members of God's family." (Ephesians 2:19)

EPHESIANS

279

Week 45, Day 4

Write About It

Sin breaks our relationship with God. And sin breaks our relationship with other people too. Read Ephesians 4:25–32. Think about the things the apostle Paul says we should and should not do. Think about one thing in those verses that you do. Write that one thing here and how it hurts your relationship with other people. Then write how you can change it.

....

....

....

God wants people to know about the wonderful life they can have by believing in Jesus. You can show people that life by how you live. What are some things you do that show people what that life looks like? Write your thoughts here.

....

....

....

Pray About It

Dear God,

Thank you for fixing my broken life. Thank you for giving me a new, better life because I believe in Jesus. He shows me what that new life is like. I know that you want other people to know about this life too. And so do I! Help me say and do things that will help them understand what this life is like. I ask you for this because I believe in Jesus. Amen.

Make a list of 10 things you could do to show others what a new life in Jesus is like. Read Ephesians 4:25–32 again for ideas.

1. _____

2. _____

3. _____

4. _____

5. _____

6. _____

7. _____

8. _____

9. _____

10. _____

281

EPHESIANS

Week 45, Day 6

Do Something About It

Sin does a lot of harm. Sin hurts our relationship with God. Sin also hurts our relationships with one another. God wants something better for human beings. People can have that better life by trusting in Jesus.

Read Ephesians 6:10–18. Did you notice these verses sound like we are in a battle? Well, that's because we are! But the battle isn't against other people. The battle is against sin and the devil. We must fight against sin and the devil by living the way God asks. God's armor has six pieces. List the six pieces of God's armor we need for this battle. Write next to each piece what it is or what it helps you do. Then draw a picture of yourself wearing those pieces of armor. Use your picture as a reminder of how you are to live. And it will remind you to tell other people the good news of Jesus Christ.

Read About It

PHILIPPIANS

God gives us joy no matter how bad things get.

When the school year is almost over, don't you look forward to summer vacation? Maybe you and your family will travel somewhere. Maybe you'll be able to go to the beach or to the pool. You'll be able to hang out with your friends. You know it's going to be great! But until the school year is over you still have homework to finish. And you still have to go to school. All of that can be hard work! But even while you're working hard in school, you know that summer vacation is still coming! That makes the work not so hard.

That's like what the apostle Paul is telling the believers in this letter to the Philippians. He tells them that they might have to do things that are hard. People might be mean to them just because they believe in Jesus. They might even be put in prison just like Paul was. But Paul tells the believers that they can still have joy. They can have joy even while all of those hard things are happening to them! That's because God's promises to them are true. They are his children no matter how bad things get. And you are God's child too when you believe in Jesus. He has wonderful things in store for you in the future! Remembering that can help you during hard times.

What kind of work feels hard to you? What kind of work gives you joy?

Think About It

Jesus will help you with anything! Write that sentence on the treasure map below. Start in the upper left corner. Then put one letter in each square. Don't put any spaces between the words. When you come to the end of one row, continue on the next row. When you're done, look at the letters in the shaded squares. They will spell out the treasure that Jesus provides for you!

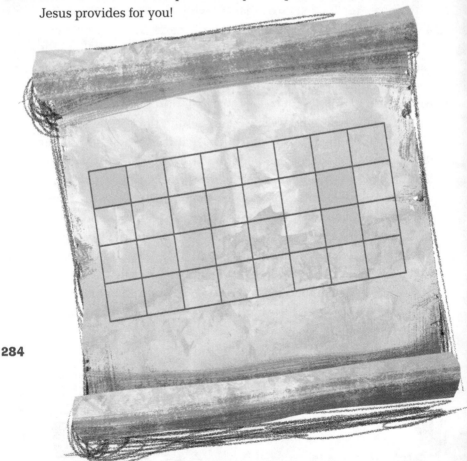

Finding Jesus in Philippians

The apostle Paul wanted the Philippians to know that they could have joy. That's why Jesus had come! When Jesus was born, an angel told some shepherds about it. The angel said, "I bring you good news. It will bring great joy for all the people. Today in the town of David a Savior has been born to you." (Luke 2:10–11)

Jesus came so we could have joy. We can have that joy by believing what he told us. He told us that when we believe in him we become God's children. And God will always love his children, no matter how bad things get. Jesus wants us to have the same joy that he had. Here is what he said in John 15:11. "I have told you this so that you will have the same joy that I have. I also want your joy to be complete."

We can have the same joy Jesus had when we remember what Paul told the Philippians. It was so important that he said it twice! In Philippians 3:1 and in 4:4 he said, "Be joyful because you belong to the Lord!" We will always belong to the Lord. So we can be joyful no matter what happens!

Color the words below to remind yourself to rely on Jesus.

PHILIPPIANS

Week 46, Day 4

Write About It

Because you believe in Jesus, nothing can take away God's blessings from you. You are his child. He will always be with you. You have a special relationship with him that will last forever. Write how this makes you feel.

....

....

....

....

Maybe you think other things will bring you joy. Why is it better to find joy in your relationship with God? Write your thoughts below.

....

....

....

....

Pray About It

Dear God,

Thank you that you made me your child when I believed in Jesus. You will always be with me and will always love me. Knowing that helps me have joy even during hard times. I admit that sometimes I look for joy in other things. I'm sorry for that. I know those other things don't last. You are the only one who lasts forever. So, your love for me will last forever too! Please help me to remember that. Then my joy will last forever too! I ask you for these things because I believe in Jesus. Amen.

Color the verse below so you can remember to be joyful.

287

PHILIPPIANS

Do Something About It

In the letter to the Philippians, the apostle Paul talks about a joy that nothing can take away.

Get a blank piece of white paper. Fold it in half like a greeting card. On the front of the card write the word "JOY." Make sure you press down hard. It might help to use a ball point pen.

Now open up the card. Using the side of a pencil, lightly shade in the middle of the right hand blank page. As you do, the shading should make the word "joy" appear! That's exactly how it is with the joy God gives you when you believe in Jesus. All sorts of bad things may happen to you. They're like the black shading on your paper. But those bad things can't keep your joy from being seen! Your joy comes from knowing that you are God's child.

Decorate your card and write the verse from Philippians 4:4 on it. Give it to someone who needs JOY.

Read About It

Jesus is greater than everything else.

Suppose you had a choice between one million dollars or one penny. You'd choose the million dollars, right? Who would take a penny when they could have so much more? That wouldn't make any sense! But some believers in Colossae were doing something that made no sense either. They were choosing to trust in other things instead of Jesus!

Some people in Colossae were saying that some things were greater than Jesus! Their words sounded good, but they were totally bogus! These people had all kinds of useless and harmful ideas. And they were trying to get the people in the church to believe them.

The apostle Paul tells the believers not to be fooled. Choosing other things instead of Jesus is always a bad idea. Jesus is greater than everything else! He is smarter and stronger. He is fairer and more patient. He is more loving and worthy of our trust. Choosing to trust in something else instead of Jesus doesn't make any sense. It's even worse than choosing a penny instead of a million dollars!

Have you ever been fooled into trusting other things instead of Jesus? Why did you do that?

COLOSSIANS

Week 47, Day 2

Think About It

The apostle Paul wanted the Colossians to recognize that Jesus is greater than everything. Can you recognize the greater thing in the choices below? For each number, circle the correct answer. Then find the number of the question and the letter of its answer on the picture below. Draw a line connecting the number of the question and the letter of its answer. When you're finished drawing the seven lines, you should see a word. You may have to look a few times before you see the word. That word will remind you of the greatest one of all!

1. What is stronger?
   a. a gorilla
   b. a lizard

2. Who is smarter?
   c. a scientist
   d. a fly

3. Who is more loving?
   e. a mother
   f. a bully

4. Who is more patient?
   g. a person who cuts in line
   h. a person who waits their turn

5. Who is worthier of your trust?
   i. a spy
   j. a pastor

6. Who is kinder?
   k. a nurse
   l. a monster

7. Who is fairer?
   m. a cheater
   n. a judge

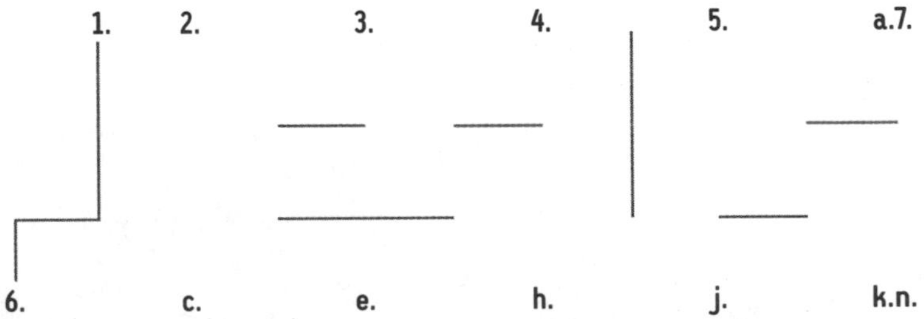

1. 2. 3. 4. 5. a.7.

6. c. e. h. j. k.n.

Week 47, Day 3

Finding Jesus in Colossians

COLOSSIANS

God wants you to know that Jesus is greater than everything else.

Paul tells believers why it only makes sense to choose Jesus. We don't have to look for other spiritual mysteries to explore. We can explore the mystery of Jesus!

Read Colossians 2:2. Write in your own words what Paul wants for the church.

....

....

....

Read Colossians 2:3. Write in your own words what Paul is saying.

....

....

....

Read Colossians 3:16–17. Write in your own words what Paul is saying.

....

....

291

....

Everything the Colossians were looking for they could find in Jesus. He is so much greater than anything else!

Week 47, Day 4

Write About It

The Colossians trusted other things instead of Jesus. Some people had made them believe that other things were better. Maybe you've started to believe other things are better too. Are you trusting in other things instead of Jesus? Write your thoughts here.

....

....

....

We often want to be like the people we think are great. Jesus is the greatest, so what does it mean to be like him? The apostle Paul describes this for us in Colossians 3:12–17. Write down all the ways these verses say we should be like Jesus.

....

....

....

Pray About It

Dear God,

Thank you for sending Jesus to us. He is greater than everything else. It doesn't make sense for me to trust in anything instead of Jesus. But sometimes I do anyway. Please forgive me and help me to remember that Jesus is all I need. Other people might try to get me to trust in other things instead of Jesus. Help me not to listen to them. Help me to keep trusting only in Jesus. I want to be more like him. I ask you for these things because I believe in Jesus.
Amen.

The T below stands for **Trust**. Inside the letter write the things in your life that you need to trust God to help you handle.

Week 47, Day 6

Do Something About It

When we really believe that Jesus is greater than anything else, we'll do what he says. The book of Colossians describes some of the things we can do. These things will show other people that we think Jesus is greater than anything else. The first step is to find out what these things are. You can find them by filling in the blanks in the verses below. After you have filled in the blanks, write down one way you will do each thing. The first one has been done as an example. Then pray and ask God to help you do it. Write down the day this week when you were able to do it. See how many you can accomplish this week.

VERSE	WHAT WILL I DO?	WHEN DID I DO IT?
Colossians 2:7 Be more thankful than ever before.	I'll make sure to thank my teacher this week.	
Colossians 3:5 Don't let your _____ get out of control.		
Colossians 3:8 You must get rid of anger, rage, hate and _____ .		
Colossians 3:12 Be _____ and _____ .		
Colossians 3:12 Put on tender mercy and _____ .		
Colossians 3:13 _____ one another.		
Colossians 3:20 Children, _____ your parents in everything.		
Colossians 4:6 Let the _____ always be full of grace.		

Read About It

**God wants us to be busy serving
him until Jesus returns.**

Have you ever taken a trip in a car? Maybe you were in a hurry to get there. It may have seemed to take a lot longer than you would have liked. You may have even said more than once, "Are we there yet?" You could only think about the end of your trip. There may have been a lot to see and do along the way. But you were missing out on all of that. You just wanted to get there!

That's a lot like the problem the Thessalonians were having. They were thinking a lot about when Jesus would return. Jesus is certainly going to return! But the Thessalonians didn't understand how they were supposed to live until that happens. There is a lot to see and do before Jesus returns! The apostle Paul wrote this letter to them to remind them of those things.

In 1 & 2 Thessalonians, the apostle Paul describes the Christian life like a farmer's field. A farmer's field should produce a good crop. The life of a person who believes in Jesus should produce good things too. For example, it should produce patience, respect, help for others, and kindness. When other people see these things, they'll want to believe in Jesus too! These are the things God wants us to be busy doing until Jesus returns.

Did you ever think of yourself as a farmer? Or did you ever think of your life as a field? What kind of good "crops" is your life producing?

Week 48, Day 2

Think About It

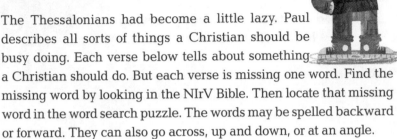

The Thessalonians had become a little lazy. Paul describes all sorts of things a Christian should be busy doing. Each verse below tells about something a Christian should do. But each verse is missing one word. Find the missing word by looking in the NIrV Bible. Then locate that missing word in the word search puzzle. The words may be spelled backward or forward. They can also go across, up and down, or at an angle.

1. That's because God chose us to live _____ lives.
   1 Thessalonians 4:7

2. And do everything you can to live a _____ life.
   1 Thessalonians 4:11

3. So _____ one another with these words of comfort.
   1 Thessalonians 4:18

4. Instead, let us be wide awake and in full _____ of
   1 Thessalonians 5:6
   ourselves.

5. Live in _____ with one another.
   1 Thessalonians 5:13

6. _____ those who are weak.
   1 Thessalonians 5:14

7. Be _____ with everyone.
   1 Thessalonians 5:14

296

8. Always try to do what is _____ for each other
   1 Thessalonians 5:15
   and for everyone else.

9. Always be _____.
   1 Thessalonians 5:16

10. Never stop _____.
    1 Thessalonians 5:17

11. Give _____ no matter what happens.
    1 Thessalonians 5:18

12. That is only right, because your _____ is growing
    2 Thessalonians 1:3
    more and more.

13. Brothers and sisters, remain _____ in the faith.
    2 Thessalonians 2:15

14. May the Lord fill your hearts with God's _____.
    2 Thessalonians 3:5

15. Keep away from every believer who doesn't
    want to _____.
    2 Thessalonians 3:6

E	L	P	U	X	D	X	S	P	W	T	G	X	H	Z
G	Q	X	R	C	J	H	T	L	K	T	E	L	D	Y
A	B	X	T	A	J	J	O	O	H	I	O	I	F	N
R	P	U	R	E	Y	R	J	A	I	V	B	J	U	N
U	W	N	U	P	T	I	N	C	E	Z	E	O	G	Q
O	W	Q	Q	N	A	K	N	H	F	S	J	Y	E	A
C	K	R	O	W	S	V	T	G	R	P	A	F	A	M
N	G	C	C	D	H	I	I	O	M	O	N	U	E	A
E	X	X	A	U	A	E	W	O	M	H	H	L	M	I
U	C	S	C	F	O	P	L	D	W	W	O	E	Z	Y
P	A	T	I	E	N	T	G	P	W	P	L	C	X	W
K	C	Y	Y	T	L	B	F	I	W	P	T	A	P	P
V	Q	D	M	V	Z	N	L	B	F	F	M	E	U	R
G	N	O	R	T	S	Z	Y	J	M	I	X	P	U	O
G	X	T	A	C	Y	P	R	S	P	Z	Y	F	N	E

Finding Jesus in 1 & 2 Thessalonians

The apostle Paul reminds the Thessalonians that they should try to be like Jesus. When believers act like Jesus, then other people can see what Jesus is like. Then they will want to believe in him too.

It's hard to be like Jesus. But Jesus promises believers something very important. He says that when we trust in him, he will help us to be like him. 2 Thessalonians 3:3 says Jesus will make your faith stronger. 1 Thessalonians 3:12 says Jesus will cause your love to grow. 2 Thessalonians 2:16–17 says Jesus will make you able to do and say good things. We can only do these things when our relationship with Jesus grows closer and closer. Then, like the farmer's field, our lives will produce all sorts of good things! Jesus calls these things "fruit." Here is what Jesus says in John 15:5. "I am the vine. You are the branches. If you remain joined to me, and I to you, you will bear a lot of fruit. You can't do anything without me." Let's grow closer to Jesus so that we can "bear a lot of fruit"!

Draw a vine with branches and fruit. On each fruit write something good you can do or say that will make you more like Jesus.

Write About It

Paul wants the Thessalonians to act like Jesus. How would you describe to someone else how Jesus acted? Do you think people would describe you that way? Write your thoughts below.

....

....

....

Think of a time when you know you didn't do what you should have. Now think of what Jesus would have done in that situation. What could you have done in that situation to be more like Jesus? What will you do in the future to be more like Jesus? Write your thoughts below.

....

....

....

Pray About It

Dear God,

Sometimes I don't think about what you want me to be doing. I just do whatever I want. But I know you want me to help people see what Jesus is like. Then they can believe in him too. Help me to see the opportunities that are all around me to do good. I know my own faith will grow when I do these things for you. And my relationship with Jesus will get closer and closer. I ask you for these things because I believe in Jesus.

Amen.

List some ideas for showing people what Jesus is like. Reading 1 Thessalonians 5:14–18 will help you with ideas.

How I Can Show People What Jesus Is Like

Do Something About It

The Bible calls the good things believers do the "fruit" of their faith. Those "fruit" or good things show the love of Jesus to other people.

Here is something you can do to help you remember to do good things. Below is the picture of an apple tree. Every time you do something good, draw an apple on it. Write what you did beside the apple. Maybe you encouraged someone who was sad. Maybe you helped your brother or sister with their homework. Maybe you said hello to someone you usually don't talk to at school. There are all sorts of things you can do. Ask God to help you to do them. See how many apples your tree can produce! As your apple tree has more and more fruit, so will your life as a believer!

301

Week 49, Day 1

Read About It

Christians should love others and set a good example as God followers.

Suppose you were taking a test in school. You answered all the questions and were about to turn it in. But all of a sudden you realized that one of your answers was wrong! What would you do? You would probably erase the wrong answer and write in the correct one! The apostle Paul wrote letters to Timothy for the same reason. There were some wrong things going on in the church in Ephesus. That church needed to erase what was wrong in their words and actions. They needed to replace it with what was right. Paul wanted Timothy to help them to do that.

In Paul's first letter to Timothy he tells them to be sure to love one another. That's because loving one another shows that we're more concerned about other people than ourselves. When we live like that, we're living like Jesus. Paul reminds Christ's followers that even if they've made mistakes they can change, just as he did.

Paul tells Timothy and us to "Set an example for the believers in what you say and in how you live. Also set an example in how you love and in what you believe." (1 Timothy 4:12)

Think About It

1 Timothy 4:12 is a great verse for you to remember. Look this verse up in your NIrV Bible. Did you notice something? Timothy was young! And Paul was telling Timothy that he could set an example for other believers to follow. He shouldn't let his age stop him from doing that! This means that Jesus can use you too. That's so exciting! Write out 1 Timothy 4:12 below and try to memorize it!

> Don't let anyone look down on you because you are young. Set an example for the believers in what you say and in how you live. Also set an example in how you love and in what you believe. Show the believers how to be pure.
> 1 TIMOTHY 4:12

Week 49, Day 3

Finding Jesus in 1 Timothy

The apostle Paul loved the believers in the city of Ephesus. He encouraged them to show their love for Jesus in the way they lived.

In John 14:6, Jesus says that he is "the way and the truth and the life." That means that anyone who looks at him can see the *way* to live. They can also see how to live out the *truth* of the Bible. And looking at Jesus also shows them where true *life* can be found. Jesus showed us all these things by the way he lived.

God is making us like Jesus. That means we should also be showing people the life God wants for them. Here is what Jesus said to the Father in John 17:18. "You sent me into the world. In the same way, I have sent them into the world." Are you ready to show people the life God wants for them?

In the frame below, draw a picture of yourself showing your love for Jesus in the way you live.

Write About It

Everyone who believes in Jesus can show other people the good life God wants for them. And that includes people who are young like you! Your age isn't what's important. It's believing in Jesus. How does that make you feel?

....

....

....

....

Read 1 Timothy 4:12 again. What are some ways you could "set an example in how you live and in what you believe"? Write your thoughts here.

....

....

....

....

Week 49, Day 5

Pray About It

Dear God,

Thank you for sending Jesus. He told us about the new life you want for us. And he showed us what that new life looks like. Please help me to be more like Jesus. Please help me set an example for other people by the way I live. Help me to show them the better life you want for them. I ask you for these things because I believe in Jesus.
Amen.

Here's something to help you each time you pray. Use Talky's hand to remind you to pray for all of the people in your life. Pray for people who need to find new life in Jesus.

Pray for your family.
Pray for teachers.
Pray for leaders.
Pray for people who are sick and hurting.
Pray for yourself.

Week 49, Day 6

Do Something About It

The Bible guides us in the right path. It tells us what is true. And it tells us how to live according to the truth. This exploration will remind you of these things.

You'll need at least four people to play. And there will have to be an even number of players. Divide the players into teams of two. One person on each team will be the guide. The other person will be blindfolded. The blindfolded players will have to find something. Put the object they have to find at the end of the room or yard. The guides will give directions to the blindfolded players so they can find the object. The first team whose blindfolded player finds the object wins the game. Play the game twice. Then each player will have the chance to be the guide and to be blindfolded.

Remember the message of 1 Timothy when you play this game. God gave you a new life when you believed in Jesus. God tells you in the Bible how to live that life. When you live like that, you are on the right path. And you're guiding other people in the right direction too! You're like the guide in the game who leads the blindfolded person. The guide helps the blindfolded person find the object. And through your example you can help people find new life in Jesus Christ!

Read About It

**God wants us to do what is right and
turn away from what is wrong.**

The apostle Paul wanted Timothy to tell people to stop doing things that were wrong. You can read about many of those things in 2 Timothy 3:1–5. Paul warns the church that the people will do bad things. Those things are like the wrong directions in a maze. Doing those things can cause all sorts of problems for you. They can keep you from having the good life God wants for you. The apostle Paul wanted to make sure the believers in Ephesus had that good life.

As Christians, we have the tools to help us live a good life. Because we believe in Jesus Christ, we can live the best life possible.

What does having the best life God wants you to have mean to you?

308

Think About It

The apostle Paul wanted to help the church in Ephesus. He wanted to make sure they didn't go in the wrong direction. He wanted to make sure that they followed the truth they had been taught. Following that truth would keep them on the right path. And it would show other people the right path too! But there are all sorts of things that can get us off the right path. The Bible helps us know the right thing to do. It helps us go in the right direction.

Can you find the right direction in the maze below? There are all sorts of wrong directions you can take. Only one path can take you safely to the end!

2 TIMOTHY

309

Week 50, Day 3

Finding Jesus in 2 Timothy

It can be hard to do what is right and turn away from doing what is wrong. In 2 Timothy 3:12 the apostle Paul describes what happens to people who try to do that. He says that "everyone who wants to live a godly life in Christ Jesus will be treated badly."

Jesus always did what was right and turned away from what was wrong. He knows how hard it is for us! To help believers do what is right he has sent us his Holy Spirit. 2 Timothy 1:7 tells us that "the Spirit gives us power and love. He helps us control ourselves." So, the Holy Spirit helps us to live like Jesus did.

Read 2 Timothy 3:14 and 15 in your NIrV Bible. Write the verses below. Did you notice how they talk about being a little child? What do you think about that? Those verses would be good ones to write on a card and hang where you can see them every day!

....

....

....

....

....

Week 50, Day 4
Write About It

Sometimes people don't do what is right. Instead, they do things that Jesus never did. The apostle Paul talks about some of those things in 2 Timothy 3:1–5. Have you ever done any of those things? What do you think of your actions now?

....

....

....

....

Have any of those things ever been done to you? How did that make you feel? Write your thoughts below.

....

....

....

....

Pray About It

Dear God,

Please help me to turn away from what is wrong and do what is right. That can be hard for me to do sometimes. Other people might even treat me badly when I try to do what is right. Thank you for sending your Holy Spirit to give me courage and strength. Thank you that the Holy Spirit can help me be more like Jesus. I pray these things because I believe in Jesus.

Amen.

Read 2 Timothy 4:5 in your NIrV Bible. How does Paul encourage Timothy? Do you see the four things he wants Timothy to do? Write these below and ask God to help you live this way.

312

Do Something About It

Talk to some older Christians that you know. Ask them to give you advice about how to live like Jesus. Write the words of each one in a thought bubble below. Put these ideas in your room so you can keep them in your mind.

Week 51, Day 1

Read About It

God wants us to show other people what the truth looks like.

Have you ever received a box in the mail? Wasn't it exciting? Before you opened it you probably tried to figure out what was inside. Maybe you shook the box a little to see if you could tell what was inside. Maybe you learned something by looking at the return address. You tried to figure out what was *inside* the box by what was *outside* the box.

The apostle Paul wrote this letter to his friend Titus to give him some advice. Titus was appointing elders in the churches on the island of Crete. Paul wanted Titus to know what he should look for in those elders. In fact, the things he should look for should be true for every believer. Paul wanted Titus to be sure that what was *inside* a believer could be seen on the *outside*. That's just like what you looked for in that box you received in the mail! What someone sees about you on the outside says a lot about what is inside. We know the truth with our heads. God has told it to us in the Bible. But sometimes we don't show the truth by how we live. The apostle Paul tells us in this book what the truth should look like. He tells us how other people should see it when they look at us.

What do you think the inside and outside of a believer should look like?

314

Think About It

Titus and the believers on the island of Crete knew the truth. But the apostle Paul wanted to make sure they also *showed* the truth. He tells us what the truth looks like in Titus 3:1–2. If we do these things, people will be able to see the truth. Then they will be able to see the life God wants for them too!

All of the words and sentences below come from Titus 3:1–2. But they're all jumbled up. See if you can straighten them out so that the truth is clearer to see. If you get stuck, you can read Titus 3:1–2 to find the answers.

1. dRimen doG's loppee ot boye lurser nad routhaitise.

_____

2. nimdeR meth to eb darey ot do thaw si dogo.

_____

3. lelT emth nto to kapes vile nights astinga yeanno.

_____

4. dRimen hemt ot veil ni epace.

_____

5. yeTh stum ridcones het esend fo hoters.

_____

6. eyhT sumt swayal eb legnet odwart neoyveer.

_____

Week 51, Day 3

Finding Jesus in Titus

The apostle Paul knew that he was asking Titus to do a hard job. Church leaders had to be able to show the truth as well as speak the truth. That's hard for people to do!

But Jesus was different than that. Everything he did showed the truth. He showed the words of God so clearly that he is even called "the Word"! You can read about this in John 1:1–5. And in John 6:38, Jesus says that he came down from heaven to do God's will. Notice that he doesn't say that he came to *learn* God's will. He came to *do* it!

The apostle Paul wants Titus to look for people like that. He wants Titus to look for people who are trying to do what Jesus did. He says that "those who trust in God will be careful to commit themselves to doing good" (Titus 3:8). When we do that, we are becoming like Jesus!

The apostle Paul had told Titus to look for a certain kind of church leader. Do you know church leaders like that? Use the frame below to write about or make a drawing of them.

Write About It

Think about a time when you saw someone doing something good. How was their behavior showing you something the Bible tells us to do? How was their behavior showing you something true about Jesus? Write your thoughts below.

....

....

....

Go back and read the sentences you figured out in Day 2. What truths from the Bible do those behaviors show other people? Write your thoughts below.

....

....

....

Pray About It

Dear God,

Thank you for giving us your truth. You tell us the truth in the Bible. And you sent your Son to show us the truth. I want to know the truth and to live out the truth. Please help me to show other people what is true about you. Help me to become more like Jesus. Then when people look at me they can see what is true about him. Then they'll want to know more of this truth too, just like I do. I ask you to help me to do these things because I believe in Jesus.
Amen.

Copy the picture of the cross below several times on a piece of paper. Then read Titus 3:1–2. In these verses, the apostle Paul tells Titus several things he can do to show the truth. Write each one in one of the crosses. Then pray that God would help you show that truth better in your life too.

Do Something About It

TITUS

Here is an exploration you can do with your friends. It will remind you to *show* the truth God has told you in the Bible.

Have each person who is playing take turns being the actor. The actor has to do something that Jesus did. Here are some of the things they could choose from.

- Tell the truth.
- Do what is right.
- Say no to sin.
- Love other people.
- Be gentle.
- Live in peace.
- Be kind.
- Encourage others.

The actor should try to get the other players to guess what the action is. The actor can't use any words. They must act out these behaviors until someone guesses the right answer. When someone guesses correctly, someone else takes a turn as the actor. Keep playing until everyone has had a chance to be the actor. The person who gets people to guess the right answer the quickest wins!

319

Read About It

God wants believers to accept one another just as he has accepted us.

Maybe you have a brother or sister. Or maybe you have a friend that is as close as a brother or a sister. There are probably a lot of ways you are different from them. They might look different than you. They might live in a different part of town. They might be stronger or weaker than you. But you don't spend a lot of time thinking about the differences. You know that the differences aren't as important as what you have in common.

That's what the apostle Paul is saying to Philemon in this letter. Philemon had a slave whose name was Onesimus. In those days, some people thought that owning slaves was okay. But Jesus changed all of that! Philemon had become a Christian. And so had Onesimus. Paul told Philemon that he shouldn't think of Onesimus as his slave anymore. Instead, he should think of Onesimus as his brother! Can you imagine that? Even people who were as different as that could now be brothers! They could be brothers because they both believed in Jesus.

God loved us so much that he sent Jesus to be our brother. And now he wants all believers to treat each other as brothers and sisters as well. If God was willing to do that, then we should be too!

Who is easy to think of as a brother or sister? Who do you have trouble thinking of as a brother or sister? What can you do about that?

Think About It

Sometimes we focus too much on the differences between us. Then we don't see what is the same. All sorts of people believe in Jesus Christ. They can seem very different from one another. But they have the most important thing in common. They believe in Jesus Christ! That means they are brothers and sisters in the kingdom of God. Brothers and sisters can have a lot of differences. But those differences aren't more important than what they have in common.

Each pair of things below seems very different. But they have many things in common too. For each pair, think of at least five things they have in common. Write them on the lines.

1. An elephant and a mouse

   _____

2. A pen and a pencil

   _____

3. Cheese and peanut butter

   _____

4. A table and a chair

   _____

5. A door and a window

   _____

Week 52, Day 3

Finding Jesus in Philemon

Can you imagine any greater difference than the difference between God and us? God is the most powerful. He knows everything. He is perfectly good. That's not like us at all! But God became a human being named Jesus. He did that so he could become our brother. Isn't that amazing! Here's how the author of the book of Hebrews describes it in 2:11

> And Jesus, who makes people holy, and the people he makes holy belong to the same family. So Jesus is not ashamed to call them his brothers and sisters.

So what the apostle Paul is asking Philemon to do is just what Jesus does! Philemon should be able to call Onesimus his brother.

And what's true for Philemon is true for us. We should be able to call any believer our brother and sister too! Sure, there will be a lot of differences between us. But we have the most important thing in common. We all believe in Jesus for our salvation.

Joinme wants you to accept the family of God. Paul wants Philemon to accept Onesimus. Below, write the names of some people whom you can accept like that.

....

....

....

....

Write About It

God became a human being to have a relationship with us. He wants us to be his brothers and sisters. Just imagine! The creator of heaven and earth wants to have that relationship with you! How does it make you feel? Write your thoughts below.

....

....

....

Do you think of other believers as your brothers and sisters? What if they act differently than you? What if they don't look like you? Think about this and write your thoughts here.

....

....

....

Week 52, Day 5

Pray About It

Dear God,

Your love for me is amazing! I am so different from you. But you became a human being to have a relationship with me. Now I can call Jesus my brother. Please help me think about other believers the way you think about me. Help me to think of them as my brothers and sisters. Please help me to do that no matter how different they are from me. I ask you to help me with this because I believe in Jesus.

Amen.

Read Philemon 6 in your NIrV Bible. This verse is a good reminder from the apostle Paul. Write out the verse in the space below. What word does Paul use twice? That word will help you when thinking about other believers. (Hint: it has 5 letters.)

....

....

....

....

Do Something About It

Onesimus was Philemon's slave. People didn't respect slaves at all. They believed slaves should serve their masters. That's the way Philemon had been taught to think of Onesimus. But Philemon had become a believer. And so had Onesimus. Now things were totally different. That's because God considers believers in Jesus to be brothers and sisters.

Maybe you know someone who doesn't seem to fit in. But if they believe in Jesus, they are your brother or sister. They are children of God just like you are. You can do something about what you've learned from this book of the Bible. You can encourage that person who doesn't seem to fit in. Let them know that you consider them a brother or sister. Help them to fit into the group. Be a good brother or sister to them. Then you'll be doing for them what Jesus has done for you! Think about how you will do this. Then write your plan below.

Week 53, Day 1

Read About It

God wants us to keep our attention fixed on Jesus.

If you're like almost everyone, you've probably tripped over something at one time or another. You might have been talking or texting on your phone. Maybe someone left some clothes or books on the floor and you didn't see them. You were looking at something else instead of where you were walking and tripped.

The author of Hebrews is writing to believers. He doesn't want them to trip in their faith. He wants them to pay attention to where they are walking. In other words, he wants them to keep their attention on Jesus. There were some people who were trying to get them to look at the old things they trusted in. They trusted in those things before they trusted in Jesus. Those things included angels, the priests, the sacrifice system, and other Jewish practices. The author of this book wants believers to keep their attention on Jesus instead. He knows that Jesus is so much better than all of those other things. Trusting in him gives us a relationship with God forever. So don't trip over other things. Keep your attention on Jesus!

What things sometimes take your attention away from Jesus? How can you help yourself pay better attention to Jesus?

HEBREWS

Think About It

Jesus helps us connect with God. Half the letters in the bridge below are filled in. Read each verse. Answer the questions. Then fill in the boxes below the number with the letters of the word in the question. When you're done, the shaded letters across will spell out what Jesus Christ is for those who trust in him.

1. Hebrews 2:8. God has put _ _ _ _ _ _ _ _ _ _ _ under his son.

2. Hebrews 1:6. God's first and only Son is _ _ _ _ _ all things.

3. Hebrews 7:19. Now a _ _ _ _ _ _ _ hope has been given to us.

4. Hebrews 1:3. The Son is the shining _ _ _ _ _ _ _ _ _ _ of God's glory.

5. Hebrews 4:14. We have a great high _ _ _ _ _ _ _.

6. Hebrews 8:6. But Jesus has been given a greater _ _ _ _ _ to do for God.

7. Hebrews 1:4. So he became higher than the _ _ _ _ _ _ _.

8. Hebrews 13:20. Our Lord Jesus is the great _ _ _ _ _ _ _ _ of the sheep.

9. Hebrews 5:9. Eternal _ _ _ _ _ _ _ _ _ _ _ comes from him.

328

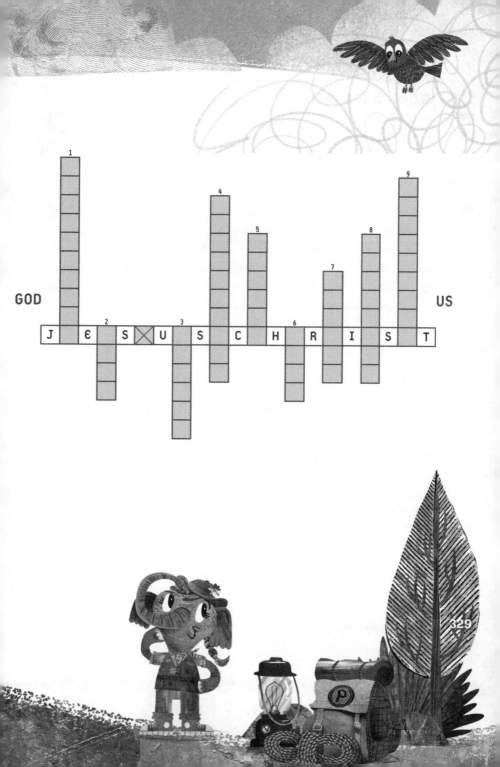

GOD

US

J E S U S C H R I S T

Week 53, Day 3

Finding Jesus in Hebrews

The author of the book of Hebrews uses the word "better" a lot. He does that to remind believers that Jesus is better than everything else that came before! Jesus gives us something *better* to believe in (7:19). Jesus brings about a *better* covenant or relationship between us and God (7:22). And this new covenant is based on *better* promises (8:6). The sacrifice Jesus made for us is *better* than all the old sacrifices (9:23). And the new kingdom that we enter when we believe in Jesus is *better* than anything else (11:16). In fact, Jesus is better than everything else! And what he does for us is better than anything we can find anywhere else.

It is better to trust in Jesus than in anyone or anything else. There are many things that people try to get us to trust in instead of him. But when we keep our eyes on Jesus, we won't stumble in our faith. That's why the author of Hebrews 12:3 says to "think about him. Then you won't get tired. You won't lose hope." And we know that God will help us do that. All we need to do is ask.

Read the five verses listed in the first paragraph above. These verses tell us about what we get that is *better* with Jesus. Write these *better* things on the lines below.

Write About It

The believers had taken their attention off Jesus. They were trying to find other ways to have a relationship with God. But there is no other way! Have you ever forgotten about Jesus? How did you realize you were on the wrong track? Write your thoughts below.

....

....

....

The author of Hebrews wanted believers to keep their attention on Jesus. He suggested all sorts of things that could help them with that. What are some ways for you to keep your attention on Jesus? Write your thoughts below.

....

....

....

HEBREWS

Pray About It

Dear God,

Thank you for reminding me of all the good things Jesus does for me. It is so easy for me to forget those things. I start trusting in other things. And then I start getting disappointed. But Jesus is so much better than everything else! Help me to keep my attention on him. Thank you for promising to help me with that! And help me to encourage other people to trust him too! I ask you for these things because I believe in Jesus.

Amen.

Keep your attention on Jesus. Write what you need to pray about in the rings of the target. Imagine hitting the bulls-eye every time you pray.

JESUS

Do Something About It

This exploration will remind you to keep your attention on Jesus. Play this game with a few of your friends. You'll need to find a tall pole or a tree. It should be in an open place where you can run without getting hurt. Take twenty long steps from the pole or tree. Then put a ball on the ground at that spot.

Now go back to the pole or tree. Each person who plays the game should run around the pole or tree ten times as fast as they can. Then that person must run as fast as they can to pick up the ball. Someone should time how long it takes them to do this. The person who can do it the fastest wins the game.

It's going to be hard to stay on track. You're going to be a little dizzy! Your body won't want to do what your brain is telling it to do! You might have a hard time keeping your eye on the ball. That's how it is sometimes with your Christian life. It's hard for us to keep our attention on Jesus. Getting dizzy and maybe even falling down a time or two will remind you of Hebrews. It will remind you to keep your eyes on Jesus!

Week 54, Day 1

Read About It

God gives us the ability to live for him when we believe in him.

If you eat cereal in the morning, this has probably happened to you. You saw the box of cereal on the table or in the cupboard. But when you picked it up, you discovered there was no more cereal in it! The picture on the outside of the box looked so good. But inside there were only crumbs. You were probably disappointed.

The apostle James wrote this letter to make sure Christians don't become like that cereal box. He doesn't want us just to say we're Christians. He wants us to act like Christians! He tells us that having faith in Jesus means living like Jesus. It is not enough only to say the right things. Believers should also do the right things. Suppose people only heard us talk about Jesus. Suppose they couldn't see that our lives were any different than theirs. Then they might wonder if we really believed what we said we did. They might wonder if believing in Jesus made any real difference to us. But suppose they see that we are trying to live according to what we say we believe. Then they'll know that what we say is important to us. And they'll see something true about Jesus by looking at us.

How do you act like a Christian?

Think About It

JAMES

In this book, James talks about all sorts of things believers can do to show their faith. In column one are things James says believers can do to show other people their faith. In column two are opposite ways to act. Match the Bible verse from James to an example of its opposite.

Column 1

1:12 Blessed is the person who keeps on going when times are hard.

2:1 My brothers and sisters, you are believers in our glorious Lord Jesus Christ. So treat everyone the same.

3:10 Praise and cursing come out of the same mouth. My brothers and sisters, it shouldn't be this way.

3:13 A wise person isn't proud when they do good deeds.

4:11 My brothers and sisters, don't speak against one another.

Column 2

A. Did you hear that person singing out of key at church? How awful was that!

B. Did you hear about how I helped Mr. Johnson today?

C. This isn't turning out how I expected. It's not fun. I don't want to do it anymore.

D. I'm going to make sure I sit by all my friends in class.

E. I just don't think he is a nice person. I don't want anything to do with him.

335

Week 54, Day 3

Finding Jesus in James

When John the Baptist was in prison, he sent his disciples to Jesus. He wanted to know if Jesus was the one God had sent to bring new life. So John's disciples asked Jesus that question. And Jesus' answer was very interesting. Here is what Jesus told John's disciples in Matthew 11:4. "Go back to John. Report to him what you hear and see." Did you catch that? Jesus told John's disciples that the good news was not just something they could *hear*. It was something they could *see* as well. That's what the apostle James is talking about. He is encouraging believers to become like Jesus! He wants us to *show* our faith too. Here is what he says in James 2:18: "Show me your faith that doesn't cause you to do good deeds. And I will show you my faith by the good deeds I do."

Crafty left his glasses behind. In the lenses, write ways that you can show your faith just as Jesus did.

Write About It

Look back at Day 2. Which list of things describes you better? Is it column one or two? How does it make you feel to know that you are showing people what you believe? Do you think you're showing them the truth? Write your thoughts below.

....

....

....

Suppose someone followed you around during the day. What would they see that might tell them you are a follower of Jesus? How could you help them see that more clearly? Write your thoughts below.

....

....

....

Week 54, Day 5

Pray About It

Dear God,

I haven't thought very much about the way I live. I know now that I show people what I believe by what I do. Jesus showed us the truth perfectly. I want to be more like him. Please help me think about this during the day. Please help me to choose to do the right thing. And please help me show the truth better with my life. I ask you for these things because I believe in Jesus.

Amen.

Show Greeny how you will show people what you believe. Write some specific plans below. For example, perhaps you can volunteer your time at a retirement village for older people. Or maybe write a special note to someone that would brighten their day. Or just help your parents around the house.

....

....

....

....

....

....

....

Do Something About It

Something can look like one thing on the outside, but be something else on the inside. This exploration will remind you of that.

You'll need an adult or older person to help you. Get a raw egg, a bowl, and a small nail. Hold the egg over the bowl. Tap on one end of the egg with the nail. Make a small hole in the end of the egg. Be careful not to break the whole egg! Turn the egg over. Make a small hole in the other end of the egg. Be sure you keep holding the egg over the bowl. You should end up with a small hole in both ends of the egg. Blow into one end of the egg. The inside of the egg should start to come out the other end! You'll have to blow very hard to get it all to come out.

When you're done, you'll be holding an empty egg shell! Take the empty egg shell to the sink and rinse it out. When you're done, carefully dry off the outside of the egg shell. Write on the egg shell with a marker: **James 2:20 "Faith without good deeds is useless."** Now put the egg shell on your desk or dresser. Every time you look at it you'll remember the message of James. An egg shell with no egg is useless. And faith without good deeds is useless if you want to show people the truth about Jesus!

HELLO! NICE TO MEET YOU!

339

Week 55, Day 1

Read About It

God gives us grace to keep trusting him during hard times.

Have you ever been blamed for something you didn't do? You probably thought that was very unfair! And it was! If you think about it, the same thing happened to Jesus. He never did anything wrong in his whole life. But people killed him anyway. That was *really* unfair! It can be hard for believers to keep trusting God when things like that happen. We might wonder if God is still in control.

That's why the apostle Peter wrote this letter to the church. The believers were living good lives. But other people were blaming them for doing wrong things. They were making them suffer. It wasn't fair! But Peter tells them they should keep doing the right things anyway. God is still in control. Here is what he says in 1 Peter 2:12: "People who don't believe might say you are doing wrong. But lead good lives among them. Then they will see your good deeds. And they will give glory to God when he comes to judge." It might be hard, but God will give us the grace to do it!

Have people ever given you a hard time for doing the right thing? Read 1 Peter 4:19 in your NIrV Bible. What does the apostle Peter say you should do when that happens?

Week 55, Day 2
Think About It

The apostle Peter encourages believers who are suffering because of their faith. In this exploration, you'll read a verse. That verse talks about how God helps you in those hard times. You are given the number of five letters in the verse. Find the letters by counting from the beginning of the verse. These letters will spell out God's special gift to keep your faith strong. Count carefully.

1 Peter 5:10

10th letter: _____

124th letter: _____

4th letter: _____

145th letter: _____

166th letter: _____

_____

341

Finding Jesus in 1 Peter

The apostle Peter wanted to encourage believers who were suffering. People were giving them a hard time because they believed in Jesus. Peter told believers they shouldn't be surprised that was happening. After all, Jesus suffered too. Here is what Peter wrote in 1 Peter 4:1. "Christ suffered in his body. So prepare yourselves to think the same way Christ did." What does it mean to think the same way Christ did? In 1 Peter 4:19 Peter says, "Here is what people who suffer because of God's plan should do. They should commit themselves to their faithful Creator. And they should continue to do good."

It can be hard when we suffer for believing in Jesus. But God gives us grace to keep trusting him. God helps us deal with our suffering in the same way Jesus did. Find the words below that describe how we can be like Jesus during hard times.

Be J_ _ _ _ _ _ that you are taking part in Christ's sufferings. (1 Peter 4:13)

They must turn away from E_ _ _ _ and do good. (1 Peter 3:11)

But suppose you S_ _ _ _ _ _ for doing good, and you put up with it. God will praise you for this. (1 Peter 2:20)

Be U_ _ _ _ _ _ _ _ _ _ _ _ _. Love one another. Be kind and tender. Be humble. (1 Peter 3:8)

Dear friends, don't be S_ _ _ _ _ _ _ _ _ by the terrible things happening to you. (1 Peter 4:12)

Write About It

Here is what Peter says in 1 Peter 4:14. "Suppose people say bad things about you because you believe in Christ. Then you are blessed, because God's Spirit rests on you." Has anyone ever made fun of you because you are a Christian? Write how that made you feel.

....

....

....

Earlier in his life Peter said three times that he did not know Jesus. You can read about this in Matthew 26:69–75. Have you ever hidden the fact that you are a Christian? What caused you to do that? Write your thoughts below.

....

....

....

I PETER

Pray About It

Dear God,

Thank you for the truth you have given to me. Please help me learn it well. And please give me your strength when I might suffer for the truth. I know that's what Jesus did for me. I want to keep saying and doing the right things. Help me to stay faithful until Jesus comes again. I ask you for these things because I believe in Jesus.

Amen.

Prayer keeps our hearts and minds focused on God. That's important to do when we suffer because of our faith. Use the chart below to track how many times you pray this week. It should be at least once a day.

Day	Time	What I Prayed About

344

Do Something About It

I PETER

The apostle Peter wrote this letter to remind believers to hold on to the truth. How long can you hold on? Here's something you can do with your friends to remind yourselves of what Peter has written.

Find a bar that you can hang from. Make sure it is not too far above the ground. You don't want to get hurt if you fall! If you can't find a bar, a low, strong tree branch could work too. Remember, you don't want it to be too high.

Now comes the hard part. See how long each one of you can hang from the bar or branch. Have someone keep track of the time. Make sure your feet don't touch the ground. It might be pretty easy at first. But it will get harder and harder! Your muscles will start to ache. Your fingers will start to slip. It will be really hard to keep holding on!

That's what Peter is telling believers. He wants us to hold on to the truth. The good news is that we don't have to depend only on our own strength. God gives us his own strength to hold on to the truth. And he has unlimited strength! So when you feel like you're losing your hold on the truth, ask God for help. He will give you all the strength you need.

345

Week 56, Day 1

Read About It

God helps us hold on to the truth as we wait for his return.

Have you been told something you thought sounded too good to be true? Maybe it was about an exciting trip you were going to take. Maybe it was about a gift you were going to receive. It was great news! You could hardly wait! But then you started thinking. What if something bad keeps that good thing from happening? Maybe your family's car will break down and you can't take that trip. Maybe the store will run out of what you were going to get as a gift. Maybe that good news really was too good to be true.

That's why the apostle Peter wrote this letter to the church. They were having a really hard time! They were being treated very badly. They thought maybe the good things they had been promised weren't going to happen after all. Peter wrote these letters to encourage the church. He tells them that nothing can keep God's promises to us from coming true. Here is how Peter describes our salvation in 1 Peter 1:4: "This is a gift that can never be destroyed. It can never spoil or even fade away." And Jesus proved what he said was true by rising from the dead. We should never let anyone or anything cause us to doubt it is true!

Do you ever doubt that the good news in the Bible is true? What can you do to help make these doubts go away?

Think About It

The apostle Peter encourages believers to hold on to the truth no matter what. In this exploration, you'll have to find and remove bad things that can get in the way of doing that. It's a reverse word search. Like a regular word search, you'll have to find the words in the list. When you find a word, color in the boxes containing the letters of the word. When you're done, there will be eight boxes left that you haven't colored. Write down the letters in those boxes in the order they appear in the puzzle from top to bottom, left to right. They will spell two words. These two words will remind you of what will remain when everything else is taken away!

U	N	K	I	N	D	W	W	T
S	E	E	N	K	R	A	D	H
T	F	L	A	W	S	N	H	S
R	E	L	T	T	W	D	S	U
O	E	U	E	R	A	E	I	N
U	R	F	O	B	N	R	L	F
B	U	N	F	D	U	I	O	A
L	G	I	A	U	V	N	O	I
E	T	S	H	E	S	G	F	R

BAD	SINFUL	WASTEFUL	SADNESS	WANDERING
EVIL	TROUBLE	DARKNESS	SUFFER	WRONG
FOOLISH	UNKIND	FLAWS	UNFAIR	

347

Week 56, Day 3

Finding Jesus in 2 Peter

The apostle Peter knew how important it is for believers to hold on to the truth. In 2 Peter 1:12–15, Peter reminds believers about the important things that God said in the past. He wants to make sure they don't forget them!

Have you heard the phrase "keep your eyes on the prize"? It means that when you are doing something, don't forget what is really important. The really important thing is the prize! God told us really important things in the Bible. What is the prize for believers? Here is what Peter says in 2 Peter 1:11. "You will receive a rich welcome into the kingdom that lasts forever."

In the space below, draw your idea of what the kingdom that lasts forever will look like. It will remind you that you'll be welcomed into a new kingdom when Jesus comes back! Knowing that will help you to keep trusting in God until then.

Week 56, Day 4

Write About It

The apostle Peter tells us beautiful truths about God. He tells us that when we believe in Jesus, we are saved. That's a gift that can't be taken away. How does knowing that you have this gift make you feel? Write your thoughts below.

....

....

....

....

Can you trust that God's word is true? Read 2 Peter 1:19–21. Write down some things you discover in these verses. Then write how knowing these things makes you feel.

....

....

....

....

Pray About It

Dear God,

Please help me hold on to the truth until Jesus returns. Sometimes people try to get me to forget it. And I will forget it if I don't read it very often. I need your grace and your power to help me. I ask you for these things because I believe in Jesus.

Amen.

God wants you to hold on to the truth! And he will help you to do it. Look up each verse below and write down what it says God has given you.

2 Peter 1:3   God's _____

2 Peter 1:4   His _____

2 Peter 1:10   God has _____

2 Peter 2:9   He knows how to keep them _____

2 Peter 3:18   Grow in the _____

Do Something About It

The apostle Peter wrote this letter to encourage believers who were having hard times. He reminded them that God would give them grace to help them get through those times. One of the ways God gives his children grace is through other believers. In fact, that's just what Peter is doing with this letter! He is encouraging suffering believers by writing to them. Here is what he says about his letter in 1 Peter 5:12. "I have written it to encourage you." You can encourage believers in the same way.

You probably know a believer who is struggling. It could be a friend or a relative. It might be someone in your church. Write a letter to them to encourage them. Think how much a letter from you would mean to them! Let them know that you are thinking about them and praying for them. Like Peter, remind them that God loves them. You might even want to write out 1 Peter 5:10 for them. When you encourage them like this, God is using you to help them in their hard times. He is using you to bring his grace to them.

Read About It

God makes us like Jesus when we believe in him.

Have you ever drawn a picture of someone? Have you ever tried to draw a picture of yourself? It can be a hard thing to do! Usually something isn't quite right. The ears might be too big or the eyes might be the wrong shape. It might be difficult for someone else to recognize the person in your picture.

That's what the apostle John was thinking about when he wrote his letters. He wanted to tell believers that they are drawing a picture too. But they aren't using pencils and paper. And they're not drawing a picture of just anybody. They're drawing a picture of Jesus! And they're using their lives to do it! But some people in the church were drawing a picture that no one could recognize. It didn't look like Jesus at all. John described for believers how to get the picture of Jesus right. John wanted to be sure that when people looked at believers, they saw Jesus.

That's what we should expect, isn't it? After all, when we believe in Jesus, we become children of God. Jesus is the Son of God. So Jesus is the brother of every believer! People who belong to the same family often behave the same way. Believers are in Jesus' family, so their behavior should begin to look like his!

What are some things that you and your family do the same way? What are some ways that what you do looks like what 352 **Jesus did?**

Week 57, Day 2

Think About It

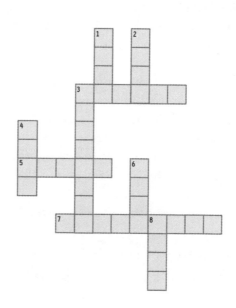

The book of 1 John talks about how to be like Jesus. Look up the verses for each clue. The verses will contain a word that describes Jesus or those who follow him. Some verses may contain more than one word that fits. Pay attention to the right number of letters.

Across

3. 1 John 2:1
5. 1 John 1:5
7. 1 John 2:1

Down

1. 1 John 1:9
2. 1 John 3:3
3. 1 John 1:9
4. 1 John 3:7
6. 1 John 1:2
8. 1 John 4:16

1 JOHN

Week 57, Day 3

Finding Jesus in 1 John

The apostle John reminds believers that we need to be like Jesus. Here is what John says in 1 John 2:6. "Those who claim to belong to him must live as Jesus did." John's three letters are full of descriptions of how Jesus lived. That's because understanding how Jesus lived will help us understand how we should live.

One way we are like Jesus is by our love for one another. In 1 John 4:16, John tells us that God is love. And God has shown us his love by sending Jesus to pay for our sins. So Jesus shows us God's love. As we become like Jesus, we will begin to love one another as well.

Another way we are like Jesus is by living according to the truth. In John 14:6, Jesus said, "I am the way and the truth and the life." If we want to be like Jesus, we'll have to learn and live the truth too. In 1 John 2:5, John says that living the truth means obeying God's word. In 1 John 2:29, John tells us that living the truth means doing what is right.

Draw some ways that you can do the following two important things.

Show God's Love

Live the Truth

Week 57, Day 4

Write About It

The apostle John talks a lot about Jesus' love for us. Even though all of us have sinned, Jesus still loves us. We can have new life now because Jesus was willing to die for us. How does that make you feel? Write your thoughts below.

....

....

....

Think about the love that other believers have shown you. What are some ways you could show the love of Jesus to them? How does knowing the truth in the Bible help you think about those things? Write your thoughts below.

....

....

....

1 JOHN

Pray About It

Dear God,

Thank you for giving me your truth in the Bible. Thank you too for showing me your truth by how Jesus lived and died for me. Please help me grow in my understanding of the truth. Help me live out that truth just as Jesus did. I want to be more like him in what I do and say. Please help me to love others the way Jesus loves me.

Amen.

The cross looks a lot like a t. That's great because we can use this image to help us remember the truth. Write true things about Jesus in the cross below. You can use some of the words you wrote on Day 2.

Do Something About It

The apostle John wrote letters to encourage believers to be like Jesus. We all like to be encouraged. Sometimes it's hard to keep doing the right things when we think no one notices. But the apostle John noticed. You can write a letter to encourage someone just like John did. It doesn't have to be long. Use the letter below to help you get started. Then write a note to someone in your life.

> Dear (Friend's Name),
>
> I've been reading the book of 1 John. He talks about how, when we believe in Jesus, we should start becoming like Jesus. I just wanted to tell you that I see Jesus in you. You live according to the truth and you show real love and care for people. Thank you for being an encouragement to me. I hope I am an encouragement to you too.
>
> Love in Christ,
>
> (Your Name)

Week 58, Day 1

Read About It

God wants us to stand for the truth and stand against what is false.

This is the apostle John's second letter to the church. In this short letter, he warns about people who are trying to fool believers. John wants to make sure that believers don't get tricked by them. These people aren't really God's children. They are telling lies about Jesus. And they don't follow Jesus' teachings. John says that's the easiest way to recognize that they are teaching what is wrong. That's because people who are really teaching the truth will follow Jesus' teachings. And those teachings say that we should love one another in the same way Jesus loves us.

In 2 John 6, what does John say it means to obey God's commands? What are some ways you can do that?

Week 58, Day 2

Think About It

2 JOHN

Did you know that 2 John is the second shortest book in the Bible? So it shouldn't be too hard for you to do this fun search! Below are ideas from some important verses. Find the verse where each idea is located and write the verse number beside it.

_____ Watch out for people who will try to trick you into believing what is wrong.

_____ God's blessing are for those who love the truth.

_____ Loving others shows that you love God.

_____ People who don't follow Christ's teaching don't belong to God.

Week 58, Day 3

Finding Jesus in 2 John

John praised people in the church who walked in the truth. If believers know the truth, they will not be easily fooled by false teachers. But some people tell lies about God's truth. And John wants to warn believers about them. He wants to encourage believers to keep living according to the truth.

Jesus is the truth. Here is what he says in John 14:6: "I am the way and the truth and the life." Any time we need to remember what is right, we should look at Jesus. Jesus is the only one who lived according to the truth all the time. People might try to get us to believe what is wrong. But we can know it's wrong if it we don't see Jesus doing it. When we live like Jesus, then we are living according to the truth. And, one of the most important ways to live like Jesus is to love one another.

How many times does the word "truth" occur in 2 John? How many times does the word "love" occur?

Write About It

In 2 John 4, the apostle John says that something gives him great joy. He says, "It has given me great joy to find some of your children living by the truth." Do you think the apostle John would have great joy if he looked at how you live? Write your thoughts here.

....

....

....

....

Have you ever been tricked into believing something that is not true? How could knowing the truth have protected you? Write about your experience here.

....

....

....

....

JOHN

Week 58, Day 5

Pray About It

Dear God,

Help me remember the truth of your Word. Help me remember that truth when people try to get me to believe what is wrong. And help me to learn and live according to the truth. Please help me to live more like Jesus. Then I will be able to love other people the same way that Jesus loves me. I ask you for these things because I believe in Jesus. Amen.

Create a picture using the verses below and hang it in your room. It will help you to remember to live the way Jesus did. Color the verse below. Always remember to walk in the footsteps of Jesus.

SUPPOSE WE WALK IN THE LIGHT, JUST AS HE IS IN THE LIGHT.
—1 John 1:7

62

Whoever follows Christ's teaching BELONGS to the Father and the Son.
—2 John 9

Do Something About It

Create at least 10 more pictures like you did on Day 5. Then add these words on each one:

Follow Christ's teaching.

Put these new pictures in places you will find them by surprise. Maybe put them in the drawer with your socks. Or maybe next to your favorite game. You get the idea. You want to come across this reminder when you aren't thinking about it!

363

Read About It

God wants us to work together with other believers to spread the gospel.

The shortest book of the Bible is 3 John. But that doesn't mean it's not important. In his final letter to the church, the apostle John is again encouraging believers. He wants them to help those who are spreading the good news of Jesus Christ. Some people were refusing to do this. John says that refusing to help other believers is wrong. We should give them whatever help we can! Here is what John says in 3 John 8. "So we should welcome people like them. We should work together with them for the truth."

How could you help other people who are spreading the good news of Jesus Christ?

Week 59, Day 2

Think About It

3 JOHN

John wants us to work together with other believers. That way more people will hear the good news about Jesus! So, we should treat other believers as friends or brothers and sisters. Read the book of 3 John in the NIrV. It's pretty short! See how many times you can find the words below.

_____ Friend or friends

_____ Believer or believers

_____ Brother or brothers

_____ Sister or sisters

_____ Church

365

Week 59, Day 3

Finding Jesus in 3 John

In this book, the apostle John writes about some bad things that were happening. Some believers were saying mean things about other believers. Some believers weren't even welcoming the people John sent to them. But John says that's not how believers should act. John wanted believers to work together to spread the gospel.

Jesus prayed for the same thing. In John 17:21, Jesus prayed for everyone who would believe in him. He said, "Father, I pray they will be one, just as you are in me and I am in you."

There is a picture of a knot below. It will remind you that Jesus wants believers to be tied together and tied to him. Write down some ideas about how believers can work together to spread the gospel.

Write About It

The apostle John wants us to help believers who are spreading the gospel message. What are some ways you could do that? Write your thoughts below.

....

....

....

....

John writes about some believers who refused to work with other believers. Those people said mean things about the other believers. Have you ever said mean things about another believer? Have other believers said mean things about you? Write about your experiences here.

....

....

....

....

Pray About It

Dear God,

Please help me to work together with other believers to spread the gospel. Help me to honor you by honoring them. And please forgive me for the times I've said mean things about other believers. I ask for these things because I believe in Jesus.

Amen.

Here is one way you can work together with other believers to spread the gospel. Get a list of missionaries from your church. Go through the list and pray for each one. You'll be helping them in their work and learning a lot too!

Do Something About It

On Day 5, you prayed for missionaries that your church supports. Now tell those missionaries that you are praying for them. Pick one or two of the missionaries on the list. Write them a letter telling them that you're praying for them. They'll be so encouraged! And you will learn about the church in another part of the world. You'll be encouraging all of them too!

....

....

....

....

....

....

....

Read About It

God warns his people about those who try to lead them astray.

Have you ever had the flu? It's not a fun time! You feel horrible and so weak. This is caused by a tiny virus that you can't even see!

Jude was warning believers about another kind of virus. The virus he was talking about is one that can make the church very sick. But it isn't a physical virus. It's a spiritual one. And it makes our faith weak. It's caused by certain people who say things that aren't true. In fact, in Jude 18 he said these people make fun of the truth. They say it's okay to sin now that we are believers. Their message might sound good to us but it's so harmful to our spiritual health! We're supposed to be becoming like Jesus.

Jude wanted believers to do two things to protect themselves against this spiritual virus. In Jude 3, he said that we should "stand up for the faith." We can do that when we know the truth. And in Jude 1 and 24, he said that we should also ask God to keep us safe. Washing our hands keeps *physical* viruses from making our *bodies* sick. And Jude tells believers what they can do things to keep *spiritual* viruses from making their *faith* sick!

Have you ever felt like your faith was "sick" or weak? How can you fix that, according to what you read in Jude?

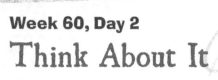

Week 60, Day 2

Think About It

Read the book of Jude. You can do it! It's pretty short.
Then take the fun quiz below.

JUDE

1. What does Jude encourage us to stand up for?
   _____
   (Hint: see verse 3)

2. What type of people have slipped in among us?
   _____
   (Hint: two words from verse 4)

3. What might some of these people do?
   _____
   (Hint: five words from verse 18)

4. What will God keep you from?
   _____
   (Hint: three words from verse 24)

5. Now for the best news of all! Write out where
   God will bring you! No hint this time!
   _____

Finding Jesus in Jude

Jude warns believers about people who want to get them to stop believing in Jesus. Jude says these people are like bad shepherds. Here is what he says about them in verse 12. "They are shepherds who feed only themselves." They don't care about their sheep at all!

Jesus is totally different. In John 10:11 he calls himself the good shepherd. Like a good shepherd cares for his sheep, Jesus cares for believers. And here is what Jesus says about his sheep in John 10:27–28. "My sheep listen to my voice. I know them, and they follow me. I give them eternal life, and they will never die. No one will steal them out of my hand." God's hand is an almighty hand! How secure do you feel knowing that his almighty hand is holding your hand? When you hold his hand, no one will be able to lead you astray!

There are two flocks of sheep below. One flock is following Jesus. Write inside each sheep something that people who follow Jesus do. Jude lists these in verses 20–25. The other flock has gone astray. They don't follow Jesus. They're trying to get the good sheep to be like them. Write inside each sheep something that people who *don't* follow Jesus do. Jude lists these in verses 16–19.

Write About It

JUDE

Your body is always in danger of viruses. You take steps to protect yourself. And your faith is always in danger of spiritual viruses. What steps can you take to protect yourself against those? Write your thoughts below.

···

···

···

Jude also reminds us that we have a good shepherd who watches over us. In Jude 1 he says, "You are loved by God the Father. You are kept safe for Jesus Christ." How does the fact that God himself is watching over you make you feel? Write your thoughts below.

···

···

···

Week 60, Day 5
Pray About It

Dear God,

Thank you for providing protection for me against spiritual viruses. You have given me the Bible so that I can understand what is true and false. Please help me to know the Bible better. And you yourself watch out for my safety. Help me come to you in prayer whenever I feel any danger. Then no spiritual virus will ever hurt me. I ask you for these things because I believe in Jesus.
Amen.

God gave us the Bible so that we can know the truth. It protects us against spiritual viruses that can lead us astray. Bible truths are like spiritual vitamins that can keep us healthy! Fill in the missing words for the important Bible truths listed below.

1. Jesus loved me so much he _____ for my sins.

2. Jesus rose from the dead and now rules from

   _____ .

3. When I believe in Jesus and ask him to forgive my sins, I

   become his _____ forever.

4. Reading the _____ helps me remember what

374   is really true and important in my life.

5. Jesus is coming _____ .

Do Something About It

Jude wants us to be able to recognize dangers to our faith. Dangers to our faith are spiritual viruses. These are things that are the opposite of what God tells us in the Bible. Knowing what the Bible says will help us recognize those dangers. Let's make sure we know what the Bible says!

Here's a game that will show you something important. It is hard to recognize a lie when you don't know the truth. You'll need at least three players for the game. Each player takes a turn telling a story. The first player will tell a story. The goal is to fool the other players! The one telling the story can choose to tell the truth or not. If they're making up the story, it should sound like it's true. If they're not making up the story, it should sound like it couldn't have happened. The listeners have to decide whether what they're hearing is true or false. Each time the other players decide the wrong thing, the one telling the story gets a point. Every player should get at least three turns telling a story. The one with the most points at the end wins.

375

Week 61, Day 1

Read About It

God will have the final victory over Satan and his evil forces.

Do you like watching baseball or football? Maybe you prefer soccer. Whatever game you like, you know that things can change at the last minute. One team can be ahead the whole game. But then to everyone's surprise the other team scores with seconds left and wins! Very exciting! And it's great if you happen to be cheering or playing for the team that wins!

The apostle John wrote this book to let believers know that their team has already won! But it sure didn't seem that way when he wrote to them. At that time believers were being treated very badly by the Romans. It looked like those who were against God were winning. But John wanted believers to know that nothing can stop God from doing what he said he'd do. God is going to remove sin from the whole earth. In fact, God is going to make a new heaven and a new earth! When God does this, all the bad things sin causes will no longer exist. Here is what John says in Revelation 21:4 about that time. "There will be no more death. And there will be no more sadness. There will be no more crying or pain."

How does reading Revelation 21:4 make you feel? Can you imagine a world without these things?

Think About It

The apostle John wanted believers to know that Jesus' team has already won! But sometimes life can be hard. It can seem like the maze below. We might not understand what is happening. It might seem like evil is winning. Will Jesus' team really win in the end? Yes! We can trust that Jesus has won the final battle already! Work through the maze to the crown of victory at the end.

REVELATION

377

Finding Jesus in Revelation

Every winning team has someone who leads them to victory. It might be the quarterback of a football team. It might be the power forward on a basketball team. Or it might be the striker on a soccer team. Believers have someone who leads them to victory too. That person is Jesus. Jesus died to pay the price for our sin. Sin can no longer have the victory over us. Here is how Jesus is described in Revelation 5:5: Jesus is "the Lion of the tribe of Judah." And this Lion has already "won the battle"!

It didn't seem like Jesus won the battle, did it? He was treated badly and then crucified! But Jesus showed he was even more powerful than the forces of evil. He did this by rising from the dead! In Ephesians 1:21–22, Paul described Jesus as sitting at the Father's right hand. Jesus sits there "far above all who rule and have authority. He also sits far above all powers and kings. He is above every name that is appealed to in this world and in the world to come. God placed all things under Christ's rule." That's the one who is leading the church to victory!

Read Revelation 5:5–14. In the frame below, draw a picture of Jesus as he is described in these verses.

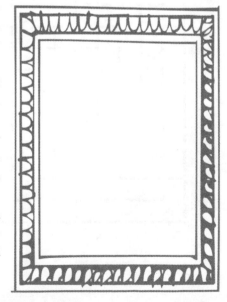

Write About It

The apostle John wrote Revelation to encourage believers who were being treated badly. He gave them an amazing picture of heaven. Read about it in Revelation 21:3. God promised to be with them and us forever. That's real encouragement! How does that make you feel? Write your thoughts below.

....

....

....

Are you looking forward to the Lord's return? Are you excited about it, or are you a bit afraid? What are you looking forward to or fearing the most? Write your thoughts below.

....

....

....

Week 61, Day 5

Pray About It

Dear God,

Thank you for sending Jesus to win the victory over sin. I know the battle is won, but it doesn't seem like it to me at times. You have such wonderful things in store for me. Please help me to wait patiently for them. Help me to trust you as I wait. Help me to trust you even when people give me a hard time for it. And help me to encourage other believers to trust you too. I ask you for these things because I believe in Jesus.
Amen.

Jesus is sometimes called the Alpha and the Omega. Alpha is the first letter of the Greek alphabet and omega is the last letter. This means that Jesus is the beginning and the end. He was there at the beginning of time and he will return at the end of time. Color this picture of the Bible to remind you that Jesus has been, is, and always will be there for you.

Week 61, Day 6

Do Something About It

One day Jesus will come again. Then there will be a huge celebration! But we can celebrate that victory now. And how can there be a celebration without cake? Here is how you can make a cake to celebrate Jesus' victory. It is just enough cake for one person. You might need an adult or older person to help you.

Personal Mug Cake

First, mix these together in a mug that's safe to use in the microwave:

- 2 tablespoons flour
- 3 tablespoons sugar
- 2 tablespoons unsweetened cocoa

Crack a large egg into the mug. Mix well.

Add 2 tablespoons milk and 2 tablespoons vegetable oil into the mug. Mix well.

Finally, add 2 tablespoons chocolate chips into the mug. If you have some vanilla, add a drop in the mug. Mix well one last time.

• • •

Put the mug into the microwave. Cook it on high for 2 minutes. As it cooks, it will rise above the edge of the mug. Don't worry! It's supposed to do that!

When it's done cooking, let it cool for a while. That's all there is to it!

381

As you eat the cake, remember why you're celebrating. Jesus has won the victory over sin. The whole earth will celebrate with you when Jesus comes again!

Genesis, Day 2

(word search grid)

Exodus, Day 2
ACROSS
1. Moses
8. ark
9. Passover
11. burning bush
DOWN
2. olives
3. Egypt
4. Red Sea
5. Nile
6. Pharaoh
7. frogs
10. Sinai
11. bricks

Leviticus, Day 2
1. burnt
2. grain
3. friendship
4. sin
5. guilt

Numbers, Day 2
1. Caleb
2. Joshua
3. Moses
4. Eshkol
5. Korah
6. Balaam

Deuteronomy, Day 2
c   g
f   b
h   e
a   d
j   i

Joshua, Day 2
We have rest because God has won the battle.

Judges, Day 2
Othniel
Ehud
Shamgar
Deborah
Gideon
Tola
Jair
Jephthah
Ibzan
Elon
Abdon
Samson
Remember to Listen to God!

Ruth, Day 2
1. Bethlehem
2. relative
3. bless, safety, care
4. family protector
5. related
6. help
7. elders
8. sandal
9. property, wife

Ruth, Day 3
1. Abraham
2. Isaac
3. Boaz
4. Jesse
5. David
6. Mary

1 & 2 Samuel, Day 2
You save those who aren't proud. But you watch the proud to bring them down. 2 Samuel 22:28

1 & 2 Kings, Day 2

(two word search grids)

1 & 2 Chronicles, Day 2
Jesus is our faithful king who brings God's blessings to us.

Ezra, Day 2

(word search grid)

Nehemiah, Day 2
no braid, no dust lines under feet, scarf is red, no lines on trunk, no flower on hat

Esther, Day 2
"You are Christ's official messengers." Tell other people about Jesus!

Job, Day 2
1. ant
2. bird
3. music note
4. paintbrush
5. hiking boot

Psalms, Day 2
1. afraid
2. troubled
3. happy
4. sadness, joy
5. glad
6. weak

If you feel strong or weak, to God you should speak.

Proverbs, Day 2

Ecclesiastes, Day 2

(maze puzzle)

Song of Songs, Day 2
Love is like a <u>blazing fire</u>. Love burns like a <u>mighty flame</u>. No amount of <u>water</u> can put it out.
<u>Rivers</u> can't sweep it away. Suppose someone offers all their <u>wealth</u> to buy <u>love</u>.

That won't even <u>come close</u> to being <u>enough</u>.

Isaiah, Day 2
Isaiah 26:13 H O N O R
Isaiah 29:13 T H E L O R D
Isaiah 43:23 W I T H Y O U R
Isaiah 38:16 L I F E

Jeremiah, Day 2
COVENANT

Ezekiel, Day 2
1. I will make my new covenant with you. Then you will know that I am the Lord.
2. I myself will take care of my sheep. I will let them lie down in safety.
3. I will search for the lost. I will bring back those who have wandered away. I will bandage the ones who are hurt. I will make the weak ones stronger.
4. I will put my Spirit in you. I will make you want to obey my rules.
5. I will make a covenant with them. It promises to give them peace. The covenant will last forever. I will make them my people.
6. I will make sure that my name is kept holy.

Daniel, Day 2
GOD IS THE MOST POWERFUL!

Hosea, Day 2
ACROSS
2. faithfulness
6. evil
7. welcome
11. safety
14. attention
15. punish
16. angry
17. obey
18. break
DOWN
1. deserted
3. save
4. guilty
5. care
8. love
9. return
10. right
11. sins
12. wandered
13. stubborn

Joel, Day 2
1. town
2. share
3. melt
4. tire
5. hurt

6. tall
7. stir
8. mile
9. youth
10. Erie

Return to me with all your heart. There is still time.

Amos, Day 2
ALWAYS BE FAITHFUL
DO WHAT IS RIGHT AND GOOD
BE HONEST WITH EVERYONE
LOVE
BE FAIR
HELP OTHER PEOPLE
BE KIND AND READY TO FORGIVE

Micah, Day 2
2. CRY → PRY → PAY → JAY → JOY
3. HIT → HAT → PAT → PAL
4. LIE → DIE → DYE → EYE → EWE → AWE
5. MAD → CAD → COD → GOD

Nahum, Day 2
1. 1:8
2. 2:1
3. 2:8
4. 2:10
5. 2:13
6. 3:1
7. 3:7

Habakkuk, Day 2
GOD IS OUR ONLY COMFORT.

Zephaniah, Day 2
B. → I.
C. → J.
N. → E.
M. → F.
C. → B.
N. → M.
F. → E.
I. → J.
A cross

Haggai, Day 2
PUT GOD FIRST

Malachi, Day 2

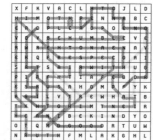

Matthew, Day 2
1. b
2. f
3. c
4. e
5. a
6. d

Mark, Day 2
Jamie had a puppy named Floppy. Jamie loved Floppy and he loved Jamie. One day Jamie took Floppy for a walk. It was a nice day in the park. And when Floppy saw a squirrel, he ran after it. The squirrel ran a long way and so did Floppy! After a while, Floppy gave up chasing the squirrel and came back to Jamie. He knew how to get back to her. Then Jamie walked all over with Floppy all that day. All her neighbors knew and loved Floppy. Jamie was happy. She wanted so much every day to see and play with Floppy again.

Luke, Day 2
The Son of Man came to look for the lost and save them. (Luke 19:10 NIrV)

John, Day 2
Hey <u>bro, the</u> room i<u>s on</u> fire!
She sold h<u>im other</u> flowers for his <u>wife</u>.
He never spreads hi<u>s tar</u> on <u>Sun</u>day.
My <u>sis ter</u>rifies her <u>friend</u>ships.
Apparently, the feet of Ka<u>te ache</u> really badly.
His <u>dirty</u> hands s<u>mudged</u> the window.
I saw <u>Tom at o</u>ne of the <u>fruit</u> stands.
By the <u>sea, the</u> beac<u>h air</u> was salty.
He purchase<u>d a dog</u> from a <u>far mer</u>chant.

Acts, Day 2
power
blowing
prophesy
bold
gift
Holy Spirit

Romans, Day 2
LEAD
LEND
MEND
MIND
MINE
LINE
LIFE

1 & 2 Corinthians
1. hot → **choc**olate
2. mean → **mean**ingful
3. break → **break**fast
4. ow → **p**ower
5. dim → **diam**ond
6. bad → **bad**ge
7. ban → **ban**quet
8. sin → **sin**cere
9. war → **war**m
10. we → **we**lcome
11. not → a**not**her
12. heat → **heat**
13. tar → s**tar**
14. hard → s**hard**
15. end → fri**end**

Galatians, Day 2
Believe in Jesus

Ephesians, Day 2
Speak the truth
Work
Say only what will help to build others up
Be kind

Philippians, Day 2
JOY

Colossians, Day 2
JESUS

1 & 2 Thessalonians, Day 2
1. pure
2. quiet
3. encourage
4. control
5. peace
6. help
7. patient
8. good
9. joyful
10. praying
11. thanks
12. faith
13. strong
14. love
15. work

2 Timothy, Day 2

Titus, Day 2
1. Remind God's people to obey rulers and authorities.
2. Remind them to be ready to do what is good.
3. Tell them not to speak evil things against anyone.
4. Remind them to live in peace.
5. They must consider the needs of others.
6. They must always be gentle toward everyone.

Hebrews, Day 2
1. everything
2. over
3. better
4. brightness
5. priest
6. work
7. angels
8. shepherd
9. salvation

GO BETWEEN

James, Day 2
1:12 c.
2:1 d.
3:10 a.
3:13 b.
4:11 e.

1 Peter, Day 2
grace

1 Peter, Day 3
joyful
evil
suffer
understanding
surprised

2 Peter, Day 2

THE TRUTH

2 Peter, Day 5
power
promises
appointed you to be saved
safe
grace and knowledge
of our Lord and Savior

1 John, Day 2
ACROSS
3. friend
5. light
7. blameless
DOWN
1. fair
2. pure
3. faithful
4. holy
6. life
8. love

2 John, Day 2
2 John 7–8
2 John 1–3
2 John 6
2 John 9

3 John, Day 2
Friend or friends—6
Believer or believers—3
Brother or brothers —1
Sister or sisters—1
Church—3

Jude, Day 2
1. Faith
2. Ungodly people
3. Make fun of the truth **OR** follow their own ungodly desires
4. Falling into sin
5. Heavenly glory

Jude, Day 5
1. died
2. heaven
3. child
4. Bible
5. again

Revelation, Day 2